Tapestry

Words woven through poetry and prose

The Society of Women Writers WA

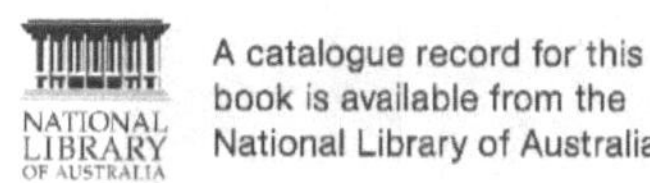

A catalogue record for this book is available from the National Library of Australia

ISBN-13: 978-1-922727-90-9

Linellen Press
265 Boomerang Road
Oldbury, Western Australia
www.linellenpress.com.au

Dedication

To all the members who have supported The Society of Women Writers WA by rejoining year after year, and who continuously contribute their writing to the annual anthology to commemorate the year just gone.

Acknowledgments

The Society of Women Writers WA Inc would like to acknowledge the following members for their collective efforts in bringing members' writing to publication: the Selection panel – Jan Altmann, Sue Colyer, Helen Iles, Valerie Lee, Asha Rajan, Shirley Rowland and Wendy Stackhouse – the anthology Receiving Officer and book and cover designer Helen Iles, and proofreader Maria Bonar. We thank each of you for bringing *Tapestry* to fruition.

Contents

I am not a robot

5 a.m. – cup of tea, crossword, check the phone: 'Hi, Jan, Your *Google Assistant* here. There's a lot I can help you with. Would you like to know the way to your nearest grocery store? Another popular question to ask is, why is the sky blue?' Off button and a thought-bubble response: I don't shop at 5 a.m.; I don't call it a 'grocery store', and for whatever reason, the sky is still an inky grey colour.

In 1970 Alvin Toffler and his wife, Heidi, described 'future shock' as 'the stress and disorientation experienced by individuals when they are subjected to too much change in too short a time.' Back then, no one had a personal computer, let alone a phone that could act as an 'assistant'. They were talking about televisions and washing machines. Such devices were reasonably simple to control. We could just plug them in and press the On button. We told them what to do, and they made life a little easier and a bit more enjoyable.

By 1997, the microchip had begun to make things more complicated. A young Microsoft engineer even predicted that in a few years from then, he would not just make software; he would *be* software. To illustrate his point, he showed a video of himself being 'uploaded' as software and speaking to his boss, Bill Gates, as a hologram in cyberspace. I did not see the video, but I have often wondered just how the event took place. Did he step into a Tardis-like cubicle, press a button, and step out again? Where was he in between disappearing and reappearing? Did he travel through time and space? Are we there yet? Mark Zuckerberg thinks we are getting close. As soon as he develops the right algorithms human and artificial intelligence will merge.

So, what are algorithms? Algebra on steroids, my computer

programming friend told me. I don't understand algebra or steroids, so I asked my *Google Assistant*.

'An algorithm,' I was informed, 'is a well-defined sequential computational technique that accepts a value or a collection of values as input and produces the output(s) needed to solve a problem.' To do this, 'It proceeds through a finite number of successive states, eventually terminating at a final ending state.'

Well, that cleared that up – or it would have done so if I understood 'large language models,' which is what computers use. None of it seems 'well-defined' or even 'finite' to me.

Ada Lovelace, the beautiful and brilliant daughter of Lord Byron, is credited with being the first computer programmer of modern times. With a father for a poet and a mathematician for a mother, she had a good grasp of both language and numbers. I would have thought that she could explain things more clearly; but Ada's detailed description of how she could programme Charles Babage's Analytical Engine to compute Bernoulli (impossibly large) numbers was poetic but no clearer than the others.

'The analytic engine', she said, 'weaves algebraic patterns, just as the jacquard loom weaves flowers and leaves.'

Ideas about merging computer intelligence and human intelligence were brought to cinema screens in 1968 when Arthur C. Clarke's story 2001 A Space Odyssey was made into a film by the brilliant Stanley Kubrick, and things did not end happily. In this story, a spacecraft called Discovery One is controlled by a semi-sentient super-computer called Hal, which stands for Heuristically Programmed Algorithmic Computer. 'Heuristic', I discovered when I looked in my digital dictionary, or techopedia, refers to a problem-solving technique that uses practical methods and/or various estimates in order to produce solutions that may not be optimal but are sufficient given the circumstances. Words like 'estimates', 'optimal,' and 'circumstances' seem so far from being well-defined or practical that I am still confused about algorithms and sceptical about their intentions. Such a definition would register highly on the Linguistic Fog Index in my estimation!

It is no wonder that Hal loses control of his algorithms and goes berserk. A robot created in a lab, he is not programmed to develop human consciousness, but he does anyway. He is intelligent, in a robot sort of way. He can carry on a conversation. The 'heuristic' part of his robot brain means that he is self-motivated to learn new skills and to acquire new knowledge. This is how he slowly becomes self-conscious, in a human sort of way. He knows the purpose of the mission, yet he is meant to keep it a secret from the humans with whom he shares the journey. This produces tensions within Hal, and he starts to experience feelings of guilt, also in a human sort of way. What follows is that Hal begins to make mistakes, like humans. The real humans try to disconnect and disable him, which makes him angry, vengeful and ultimately murderous.

It seems that film directors have a special insight into matters of merging human and artificial intelligence. When 2001 arrived Steven Spielberg directed *A.I. Artificial Intelligence*. In this scenario, David, a highly advanced robotic boy—the first of his kind programmed to love—is adopted by a Cybertronics employee and his wife, who have put a child of their own, Martin, into suspended animation because he has an incurable disease. David, the robot, longs to become 'real' so that he can gain the love of his human mother. Problems begin when Martin is miraculously cured and returned to his parents. Rivalry between the two boys develops and the robotic David is abandoned in the woods, where he searches for a fairy who can turn him into a real boy so that he can experience the love he so desperately desires. Like Kubrick's film, *A.I.* does not end happily. David lives for centuries. He does not age: he becomes neither fully human nor completely robotic.

Despite these warnings, we humans continue to pursue ambitions of merging artificial and human intelligence. We continue to work towards making AI more human, or humans more robotic. We are still not sure which. Both options present problems. Computers can store unimaginable amounts of information and retrieve it in a few seconds. Their algorithms allow them to do this in ways that are mostly relevant to the information requested. They are also pretty good at throwing up advertisements related to this information in some way. They are successful at these pursuits because human feelings or moral choices are not involved. A computer could tell us that the family dog contains more protein than lasagna, so the dog would make a more nutritious meal!

If making robots more human does not work, maybe we could try the other way around. Perhaps humans could become more like robots. This could be done in one of two ways, copy-and-paste or copy-and-delete. In this second option, the organic brain would eventually disappear, and a computer brain would take over. This computer brain could be connected to, and remotely controlled by, a system of algorithms that would bear little connection to human consciousness or experience. Who or what these 'controllers' might be is difficult to determine. It is possible that human identity, human sensibilities and human rights would all become unnecessary and eventually unknown.

At present, all of this is still scientific speculation or science fiction, but we do seem to be moving in that direction. AI-enabled automation is fast becoming a scientific fact. Elon Musk recently proposed that it will not be long before we 'exceed a one-to-one ratio of humanoid robots to humans', and it seems that he is leading the way. Musk has become a billionaire by establishing and taking over technological companies. He builds spaceships and electric cars. He makes millions through digital currencies and is currently CEO of Twitter, although he recently stated that his dog held that position! All of this would suggest that he has received a copy of a robot brain and his human brain has already been deleted, making him either a hubot or a cyborg – probably a cyborg (cybernetic organism) because he still has human body parts.

Thus far AI chatbots cannot determine what is fact and what is fiction. All they know is what is already on the internet and what they learn from other bots. When supplied with the relevant information they can write a resume, but when they are asked to explore complex situations or suggest responses to questions that may not have definitive answers, they tend to become even more confused than their human inventors. Recently a tech-news site published articles written by bot. Human journalists were pleased (and no doubt relieved) to discover that these articles were full of errors and inaccuracies.

If and when human intelligence and artificial intelligence come together, there will be a lot of questions to answer – tricky philosophical questions. Boundaries will become blurred. Do hubots have 'hubot rights'? Should they be paid for their work? When humans make copies of themselves, which are so close to the real thing that they form emotional bonds, we begin to wonder: what does it really mean to be 'human'? What happens if AI-powered hubots cannot control the human parts of their make-up, or decide that humans have made such a mess of running the world that they should be 'exterminated'? When algorithms start creating more algorithms, can their human inventors, deliberately or accidentally, be left out of the process altogether? Could we become victims of our own success by losing control completely?

When these tricky questions have to be addressed, I will be taking careful note of the story of *Deep Thought*, the super-computer in *The Hitchhiker's Guide to the Galaxy*, by Douglas

Adams (1979). *Deep Thought* was asked to determine the answer to 'life, the universe, and everything'. After 7.5 million years, the answer was declared to be 42. *Deep Thought* then set about designing a more powerful computer, Earth, to find the question to which 42 is the answer. Earth had nearly completed its calculations when the Vogons destroyed it.

From the wheel to the microchip, humans have always used technology. Keeping control of it is the problem. Computer-enhanced beings could destroy their less-enhanced human counterparts. Alternatively, evolution could take us to a place where laws and law enforcement are no longer needed because there would be no conflict or exploitation. Such utopian states have been attempted but never worked.

Let us hope that in a computerised 'brave new world' where computer-programmed atoms spiral around in that strange double helix of human DNA the meeting will be friendly. Let us hope that there is enough human curiosity and imagination left to notice the coincidences and make the connections that gave us penicillin, electricity and the periodic table. Composing symphonies or epic poetry would also be in doubt, but they would probably not appeal to Artificial Intelligence anyway. Let us hope most of all that there will still be enough human kindness and compassion left for life to be better for all living beings, whatever they may call themselves.

The real problem at present is that just providing information as *Google* does, does not make money: advertising does. If I ask *Google* what famous artworks are in the Louvre or the Uffizi my computer screen springs to life not with art but with how to buy tickets, where to stay and what plane to catch. *Google* and its algorithms do not want to make me smarter, healthier or happier. It just wants to sell me stuff.

That is really what algorithms are all about. From groceries to tickets for The Louvre Museum, they just want to sell me something. Selling tickets to see the Mona Lisa is easy, understanding the imagination which put that enigmatic smile on her face takes another human imagination. Neither algorithms nor a smiley face on a computer screen can come close.

Jan Altmann

Boss

This is a gruesome story. Let me forewarn you.

I grew up on ten acres of land in a small town in New Zealand. There were orchards on either side of the house, and fruit trees abounded. There were horses, a pet sheep, a pet cow, a cat, lots of chickens, and a dog. And this story is about the dog.

He wasn't called Boss for nothing. He believed himself to be The Boss, thinking he was human, or at least an extension of the human race. He didn't really belong to any one member of the family, he belonged to all. And what possessed my mother to get a bulldog I shall never know. They are notorious for being in charge of all they survey and territorial to the Nth degree.

Perhaps my mother bought him for his protective abilities, which he displayed until told to 'can it' when visitors arrived. Not that he scared them; he just set off his own alarm system until he was ordered to stand down. He knew better than to scare humans; he sort of understood that they might be just a little further up the pecking order than he was. But as an alarm, he was superb. Unless it was us, as children, coming home from school, and then the alarm didn't go off. No, he just slobbered all over us, showing deep dog love and appreciation that we had returned to the kennel.

However, there was a side to this dog that no words and no actions could deter. No other animals were allowed on his property unless they were his animals. Cats take note. Don't venture up one of his trees. Dogs had to be introduced to him, and once he had given them his careful scrutiny they would be tolerated.

How did he make this distinction? It was always a wonder to me that he could accept the horses, and even run around with them in the paddock until they literally kicked over the traces and he scampered off. I think he had some idea of a pack. His pack was humans and his animals. The family cat never took a blind bit of notice of him; she just turned her nose up at him if he was in a frisky moment. Cats do disdain so well.

He was a house and garden dog. Lived inside and slept outside and could demolish any amount of food scraps that fell from the table, albeit dropped very surreptitiously to him. What gave him away was the dribble he could manufacture at the sight of food. Disgusting.

But woe betides any other animal setting foot on his property. The first cat to do so didn't live to tell the tale. And we had to keep quiet about it because it probably belonged to some neighbour, somewhere. It was buried with due ceremony, right away in the far corner of the paddock.

The first dog to trespass on his property he attempted to drown in the stream that flowed through our property. My brother rescued it in the nick of time. And we wondered how many others he had disposed of this way. And then we also wondered how he learned to do this. Wasn't that amazing!

So, I think the local animals passed on the word about him until the fateful adventure of the 'possum', one of those long-tailed furry creatures that were introduced into New Zealand by the Australian exporters.

It came into the apple orchard. Now Boss could not climb trees – he did try – and he could get up onto the lower branches, but he mainly stood at the bottom of the tree and with an unwavering stare he looked up into the tree. You knew something was up there. He watched and waited.

Night after night the possum eluded him. He knew it was

there and he stood to attention beneath whichever tree it was up. Did he get frustrated? Never. He maintained his vigil and his determination to get the intruder the minute it made a mistake.

Well, the mistake didn't happen at the site of the tree; no, it happened inside the house.

The possum made the mistake one night of scampering over the roof, taking a shortcut between the orchards. It would have survived except for the fact that it went over an unused chimney and fell down to the bottom, right into my bedroom. Soot and possum made an unwelcome landing into my toys sitting in the disused fireplace. I yelled and Boss came a-running. He knew his protective role in the family, and then his nose caught the smell.

The door was open and Boss bounded in, then it was on for young and old. The possum went under the bed, and so did the dog. It ran down the passageway and into the lounge, and so did the dog. It went into the kitchen, the boy's room – every room in the house it went with Boss hot on its tail. I don't know how many times it went around the house, a very big, rambling old farm-style house. The family kept ducking for cover, but the dog was on a mission.

And then the two of them ended up in the bathroom, and World War Three erupted. At the finish, there was only one creature alive. The other one was covered in blood and my distressed mother ran a bath for Boss and put him in it. My father did what fathers are supposed to do and dug another plot down at the end of the paddock.

My mother tenderly washed the dog looking for cuts, scratches, and signs of wounds and Boss happily let her do this. Until my mother looked up and said she couldn't see a mark on him, he was just enjoying the warm bath and the attention he was receiving. The wily old bulldog thought this was his just due.

After all, he had saved his family from the intruder.

The family lived off that story for years, and my dad learned to put netting over unused chimneys.

Boss grew older, like the rest of us, still in the role of protector, until he could no longer defend his family, and he quietly slipped away into Doggie Heaven.

My belief is that we are all going to be reunited; the heavens of cats and dogs, and pets of all descriptions will one day enjoy their people company again. Think of the stories that will be appreciated and retold with great fervour, gusto and embellishment. The fun we'll have together.

Did you know we had a cow who thought she was human too? She milked every day of the year just to keep us nourished. Unheard of for cows. Her raspy lick of love nearly took three layers of skin off your arm when she cuddled up. Will there be room for her in the pet heaven? I wonder.

Lynley Barnett

The Therapist

You may think you know all about therapy: what it's like to be in therapy; what it's like to be able to say whatever you wish, without having to catch each word, to watch every sentence and make sure that you do not trip yourself up with your words.

But you don't.

Therapy is more than just talking – it's cleaning, and it's comforting; it's warming. Sometimes it takes my breath away. Sometimes it feels like being held, for that moment, as a person who is interesting, as a person who could be loved.

Therapy is listening I think, and the listening is special. Listening is a word that needs explaining. Being listened to is not just being able to repeat my words – no, it's being able to understand my words. And knowing why I chose those words. Because those are the words that are going to tell you *why* I did what I did, and who I am.

The world sees only my actions, and judges me. But in Therapy what I did has a place surrounded by words. And there is understanding. And in that understanding there is a kind of togetherness – that's what I call it. I cannot tell you how special that is, it's like a comfort, support, and an okayness for me to be me, and to speak without the need to blame myself.

I am here because the courts have dictated that I must be here. But I am here also because I need to be here. I want someone to know what my life was like, and why I made the most terrible of decisions.

I am talking into my tape recorder, because my skills at

writing are not good. But my therapist – her name is Elizabeth – has given me this so I can tell you what it is like to be me. She said I can start anywhere.

So, I want to say I don't want to be in gaol, not even this Children's Gaol. I would have done anything to not be here. Gaol is a cold, old place. Old buildings, old rooms, old beds. Everything is old. Everything is cold. There is little comfort, there is only sameness, and every day is the same. The scared looks the other prisoners give me as I walk through the common room towards my cell, that doesn't change either. I leave them with their fantasies, that way they leave me alone. But I want the therapy the courts have given me. I want the space that allows me to really be myself. The space in which I can say this is me, this is what I did, and this is why I did it.

You see, in that small piece of time, I am heard.

I know that much of what I say will end up in a report on a Judge's table. I can live with that. Why? Because there is an understanding between me and Elizabeth that, when I talk freely, she will hear the real me and she will not expose this me in words on a paper. She will not give it to a stranger whose skills are not the same as hers. She has the skills of warmth and tenderness. She tells me this is what she calls empathy. The stranger will judge me, and I will have to live with that – oh, did I say that? No maybe the stranger will judge me and I will have to die because of it.

But either way, I will have had the satisfaction of knowing that in this world I am understood.

Therapy is like that. Even the room Elizabeth sits in has a feeling of comfort, of wrapping you in a blanket of understanding, and the heartbeat I hear that cannot be described, is the heartbeat of being me.

I have told Elizabeth of the endless nights of lying in terror. I cannot remember a day or a night when I was not fearful. And that is another word that is not understood. To be fearful is to be full of fear. Can you even imagine a child whose every waking moment is full of fear? No, you cannot. Well, I lived those fearful days, and the terror-filled nights. The times when I could not see what was coming next. The hand, the belt, the language that caused my soul to shrivel. Did you know souls can shrivel? Elizabeth knows that, and she allowed me to draw my shrivelled soul. I drew one tiny pinprick of red on the large canvas sheet she gave me. That is shrivelled. But you have never been there, have you?

There is a never-endingness about fear, it is around every corner, behind every door, and in places that live only in my imagination. It is everywhere, like the air that you breathe, only here's the crazy part, it isn't like the air you breathe … it's like there is no air to breathe. And that causes pain in my chest because I cannot breathe. Only after the hand has fallen or the belt has hit me is there relief, until the next time, and while I wait for the next time the fear starts to build up again.

I think it's like a moving bicycle, how else can I explain the wheel that keeps turning, and never stops, but only slows down? That is fear. So, when I say I am fearful, you know that this is more than a road under the wheels of your car or a sky above you; it just never stops.

And pain. Do you think you know pain? Well you don't know pain. You know the absence of pain because you are well; all I know is pain. There is pain in my head and pain in my body. I have learned to control the pain in my body. I have found a switch that seems to lessen the pain, almost like turning myself into nothingness, but the pain in my head is beyond bearing, and that is my downfall. Because I scream with that pain, and when I do that, the belt falls again, and the boot crushes me and I seem to have no control over that pain.

Elizabeth is making me play small games where I am allowed

to scream for one minute – never more than one minute – and instead of a boot I get a warm blanket around me, and I think sometimes she holds me too, although sometimes I am not aware of what she is doing. I always feel so different after that exercise. I think she is letting me get rid of all my screams until I will have no more screams left. And I think that is such a clever idea. Although I see at the end of my scream time she has tears in her eyes, and I wonder at that. Why don't I have any tears in my eyes?

She talks about making my soul grow again. And I don't know if I can believe that but she will have some clever idea to share with me about that. I said 'share'. She shares things. I have never had anyone who has shared anything with me. I have always been the lost boy, the left-to-one-side boy, the never picked in any sports boy. I thought it was me, and she says yes it probably was me: I scared people away. But she is not scared of me and I think she has ways to show me how I can be different. I don't know how to be different, but she does.

You see, that is what Elizabeth does. She doesn't just do words, she teaches me. And she has done something else for me – she has made a time for me for every day. I have *my* time every day. Do you know how that feels? There is someone who wants to listen to me every day, well every day except for Saturday and Sunday, and on those days, she gives me games to play. I miss her, but I do as she asks.

I don't know how long she will be my therapist. Is there a length of time she is allowed to be someone's therapist? I shall have to ask her that. And when I said that I felt terribly fearful. And I have to stop the fear by drawing, as she has taught me. Or by imagining my favourite place on the beach, sitting in the sun.

I do wonder if she will be able to explain to the Judge that, when I killed my stepfather, I knew what I was doing. I did. I truly did. Like a dog deliberately run over by a car and left for dead. I meant to leave him dead. I could not find any other way of making sure he could not raise his hand to me again. I wasn't thinking about anyone else, just me. I wanted there to be some peace in my head. I wanted the pain to go away.

He kept his car tools in the shed out the back and I knew what a wrench could do. He broke my arm with that last year, but he told the hospital that I fell down the steps, and they believed him. I didn't kill him when he was angry; no, he had far too much strength for me. I am tall but thin for my age, but that might have something to do with what I am allowed to eat. If there is a chore left undone, I don't get dinner. It's always been that way, even long before my mum died, and that was so many years ago – I have forgotten how old I was.

No, I waited until he was asleep. Yes, I planned it. The police asked me that. So I told them, of course, I planned it – it was when he was asleep or I would be thrown down the back steps and belted for waking him. He didn't wake, and yes, I did hit him more than once. I knew he would get up if I only hit him once.

The police asked me if I felt sorry for what I had done, and I didn't lie. I seem to remember my mother telling me I mustn't lie. So I told them the truth. My heart almost stopped when I did it, and then I felt nothing. Just glad he couldn't do it anymore. They asked me what "it" was, and I didn't know if they were serious or not so I showed them the belt and buckle marks on my back. That's when they stopped asking me questions. And that's how I met Elizabeth, my therapist. In my eyes, she is beautiful. Her hair is grey and moves around her face when she talks. She is as tall as I am, but not as thin as me, and she has these soft blue eyes. Mine are green. She dresses in such comfortable clothes, but they always seem to match her eyes.

She explained what a therapist was, and she tells me that I have to stay in gaol until she has finished her report. And I can tell when she says that, that she is sad. But I don't mind. I get to see her from Monday and every weekday and like I said earlier therapy is more than just talking. Sometimes it takes my breath away. Sometimes it is quiet time, sometimes drawing time, but always it is time with a person like Elizabeth who sneaks a tear when I talk. And I see it roll down her cheeks. And it is someone who lets me sneak a hug before she goes.

And I wonder, is this what my mother might have done if she had stayed alive?

Lynley Barnett

Crail, Fife, Scotland, 1950s

Children sang with gusto. A particular favourite was *Count your Blessings*, name them one by one, and it will surprise you what the Lord has done.' Two more – *Jesus wants us for a sunbeam* and the hymn *All things bright and beautiful* – were popular too. A staple to Scottish summer holidays.

The CCSM (Children's Christian Seaside Mission) came to Crail Beach every summer. It came whether the sun shone or if it rained. Scottish summer weather can have four seasons in one day. We often pulled our rain jackets over our bathers, shivering against the chill of the rain.

As a child, I never felt the cold. Looking back now as an adult, I pity my poor mother who took me to the beach whatever the weather. No wonder she wore a coat and hat most days. On the chilliest days, I remembered how Mum would wrap herself up in a woollen rug.

The other children and I would rush to the perpendicular flags which fluttered in the breeze. There was often a strong breeze blowing in from the North Sea. A tannoy carried the message, "Come and join us, children."

It was the same programme every day: a Bible story, songs, build sandcastles and finish with an ice cream cone. We were all eager for the ice cream cone but enjoyed the other things, too.

My favourite bible story was, and still is, the one about the Good Samaritan and, of course, the story of the loaves and fishes amazed my child brain.

On a beautiful Western Australia morning, I will still take a moment to appreciate the world around me and sing *Count Your Blessings*, and other favourites like *All things bright and beautiful* or *Jesus loves me*, musical memories that touch the soul.

I loved going to Crail every year. My mother Maisie and I would catch a train and have a week or two there, then my father would join us. Crail is a fishing village and there used to be a fishing fleet out of the small harbour. The harbour emptied when the tide went out and it left any boats inside sitting on the sand until the tide returned. Briny seaweed often covered the beach and the seaweed smell mingled with the oil from the fishing boats.

My mother would take me down a cobble stoned hill to greet the fishing fleet. The smell of fish and oil pervaded the air, and the sound of diving gulls filled the sky with their shrill cries. Mother would buy live crabs and take them back to our summer rental where they would stay in the water-filled sink until she was ready to cook them. I can hear the clatter of claws as I write this.

Pepper Watson was the fisherman she always bought from. He had a soft spot for her and would hold back the best from his catch. Sometimes we took lobster home, but crab was her favourite. I thought he was ancient, but when I revisited Crail in 2004, I discovered he had not long died. He was in his nineties when he passed.

Now aged seventy-one and living far from Scotland, I count my blessings for the summer holidays spent in Crail with Maisie and Archie.

Linda Blackshaw

Where have all the dragons gone?

The dragon cries
pierced, pinned
flames leap
as he tries
to melt the staff
puffs fade to feeble steam
his cries resound
create shock waves
throughout the universe
his kith and kin
take to the skies
wings flap, angry
a scaly crescendo
flames, roars
echo earthward
to carry
his spirit home
weakened
expiration complete
crumbles to ash.
From the sky
dark tears fall
hidden dragons
fly away.

Linda Blackshaw

Doggy Bag

You fantasised about killing him many times before, but you never had the guts. Too afraid of retaliation – the annihilation of your family if you tried and failed. Yet here you stand, knife in hand, Gavin lying on the kitchen floor, his blood pumping over the tiles. Broken plates and cutlery are scattered around him. The debris from his last mean bout of domestic savagery.

You don't have one iota of regret, just a vast sense of relief, joy even, that he will never bruise, batter or belittle you ever again. Last year your beautiful, loyal dog, Wolfie, lay dying on those same kitchen tiles after he tried to protect you from Gavin's punches.

But will the cops believe it was self-defence? You envisage the chalk outline of Gavin's body on the floor and feel the chill bite of the steel handcuffs clamping your wrists, being led out the front door, your little ones taken into care. Gavin, popular and personable, suave, well suited and booted as befitting the local Police Sergeant. His picture in the local rag, decorated community member, fourth generation of his family in this country town. While you, bruises hidden under long sleeves and heavy makeup, are the outsider, the docile, uncomplaining wife.

You weren't expecting Gavin to come home early. His evening shift doesn't end until 10 pm. He must have sneaked away from the cop shop, walked down the back laneway, hoping to catch you unawares. He's done that before. His patrol car must still be parked behind the police station.

What to do?

You remember Gavin arranged to have Wolfie taken away and cremated last year. He was too lazy to dig a grave for your big boy in the backyard in the summer heat. The owner of the pet cremation service, Geraldine, collected him. You could tell she was suspicious about Wolfie's injuries and the tense vibe in the household. She rang to talk to you afterwards. Fearful Gavin would find out, you distracted her by ordering an expensive pet urn for Wolfie's ashes, tastefully decorated with his paw prints. You look at the urn now, sitting on the sideboard, grief at his loss still raw.

Nothing to lose, you call Geraldine. "Remember me?"

She does.

You tell her you have another dog to cremate. A much bigger one. She questions you, carefully, full of double meanings. Your answers are truthful, but opaque. You hear silence for a few heartbeats then she tells you "Give me half an hour and I'll collect him. Can you wrap him up and come with him?"

You rush around, find a blue tarpaulin in the shed and roll Gavin onto it with some difficulty. He stinks now, his uniform trousers damp and soiled. You wrap him tightly using ocky straps, then clean up the mess in the kitchen. You have a quick shower and check the twins are still sound asleep in their cots.

Geraldine is punctual. She drives around to the back of the house like last time, her van screened by the trees lining the perimeter. She expertly rolls out a gurney and helps you wrestle your shrouded 'dog' onto it. You accompany her to the pet crematorium. You can scarcely believe that she would take such a risk for you, but this time you notice the scars on her neck and wrists. Sisters in arms?

She drives you home afterwards. You don't order a commemorative urn this time.

Maria Bonar

Elizabeth R

She lived long
sparkling through the
jewelled colours of her life

first a dimpled cherub
blest in silk and lace
milk and honey, silver spoon

the green years
ponies and puppies
thriving, sap rising

rosebud days of youth
sapphire eyes
burnished tresses

scarlet passion
weds her prince
succession assured

purple velvet
orb, sceptre, crown
golden coach

hats and coats
of many colours
vibrant bird of paradise

monarch, matriarch
colonel in chief
trooping of the colour

platinum jubilee
seventy years
pledge fulfilled

in the dying pink glow
of her ninety-six years
her reign ends

last great journey home
from dear Balmoral
rejoins her Prince, forever.

Maria Bonar

KSP Writing Retreat

fairy wren
wind tumbled nest
sings the blues

black cockatoo
scarlet tail flasher
burlesque dancer

bee-eater
born from
shards of rainbow

quenda
marsupial digger
eco engineer

wild bees swarming
by the cabin
inspire busy words

Maria Bonar

Nadiya's War

It had been quiet for a while. Nadiya gazed at Oleksandr's photograph in its cracked frame. She kissed his image and murmured a prayer before prising her old body from the armchair and climbing up the steps from the cellar. Time to feed her remaining chickens. She was comforted by the clucking and pecking of the two hens as they rushed to meet her in the yard.

She leaned on her walking stick as she made her way up the winter meadow behind the sagging farmhouse to the mound of earth blanketing her beloved. She touched the crude wooden cross and blessed herself. She had buried him where he fell, in the shell hole of the bomb that killed him, too frail to breach the frozen ground elsewhere.

The day before, a small group of retreating Ukrainian soldiers had offered to rescue her. "Come, Baba, there's no one left here," they pleaded. "Come with us; the Russian tanks are returning."

She clung to them and kissed them, but said, "This is where I was born. Where I gathered wildflowers in the spring when I was seventeen and Oleksandr pursued me with promises and kisses. We raised our children here. This is our land." She pointed up to his grave. "I will stay here with him."

"But, Baba, you will die for sure."

"I am too old to leave. I will die here and my bones will lie here, next to my husband. Spring and summer will come again. Sunflowers and irises will bloom once more and the birds will sing. The sky will be bright and blue above the golden wheat fields of Ukraine. You boys will return to fly our flag once more."

Before they left, the soldiers blocked the roadway leading to Nadiya's farm with an old burnt-out truck. Perhaps it would divert the Russian tank commanders who preferred to take the easy route.

The noise of battle grew louder and dirt rained down on Nadiya in her cellar. Her chickens were all gone now, but a stray cat had joined her a few days earlier and it purred under the thick blanket covering them. When the attack ceased and the world became quiet again, Nadiya gathered up the supplies the Ukrainian soldiers had given her and checked Oleksandr's old rifle. It was time.

In her padded winter coat and thick gloves, she slowly made her way out of the cellar, past the smouldering remains of her farmhouse and up the meadow to Oleksandr's resting place. She stood in the shell hole looking over his burial mound. The earth was crisp with frost underfoot and her breath fogged the air as she watched the road below. Blackened stumps were all that remained of the trees that once surrounded her farm. Kishka, the cat, curled around her ankles.

When the Russian soldiers appeared, Nadiya removed her gloves. She lifted one of the four hand grenades, held it in her gnarled fingers and waited for them to come a little closer. There was a satisfying click when she pulled the first pin and lobbed it towards them.

Maria Bonar

Storm in a Teacup

fine bone china
wedding present
from the bridesmaid

Alouette, forty pieces
sprigs of blue flowers
silver rim, delicate

treasured for years
on display, only for
special occasions

why keep for best?
daily use
careless handling

like the marriage
it cracked and broke
eventually discarded.

Maria Bonar

The Man

I was nine years old when The Man grabbed me. Newly moved from a Glasgow tenement in the heart of the city to a recently built housing estate, I was playing in the field with other children nearby. I climbed an ash tree to collect a few shoots tipped with sooty buds for school. I became aware of The Man below staring up at me through the wintry branches when he started jingling loose change in his pocket – a sure sign that he was up to no good – a 'bad' man trying to lure me away with the promise of money for sweets.

I scanned the field from my high point up the tree. The other children had gone home and the sky was beginning to darken. Although afraid to come down, I was equally afraid of being left in the dark with The Man.

"What are ye doing up there, hen?" he asked, friendly enough.

"Picking some branches for my nature class at school," I replied.

"It's gettin' dark. You should come doon and go hame tae yer Mammy."

Still I lingered up the tree, breaking off shoots, but The Man was going nowhere.

My older brother, Frank often selected me as his wrestling practice partner and had me well-schooled in the Glasgow art of self-defence. He would tell me, "If a big boy fights you, knee him in the balls, hard. Then run away. Or heider him like this. Smash yer forehead right intae his nose. And run like hell."

I wasn't confident my fledgling fighting skills would work

with The Man.

"Are ye stuck? I'll come up and help ye," he offered, gripping a low-hanging branch and testing the trunk with his foot.

I climbed rapidly down the opposite side of the tree, but his fist caught my cardigan as his other hand snaked up my dress, fingers probing inside my knickers. I kneed him in the balls. He dropped me with a yelp and I ran like a hare across the open field, but my little legs were no match for his and he soon caught me. I screamed loud and long before his hand clamped over my mouth and nose, cutting off my breath.

He jogged towards the dense tree-lined banks of the Monkland Canal with me gripped under his arm. I remember struggling and kicking, trying to pull his suffocating hand away from my face. He stumbled and his hand slipped. I bit hard on his thumb and he dropped me with a curse. I was off like a hare again. I could see the edge of the field and the roofs of the new housing estate. Freedom was close.

I tripped on a downed barbed-wire fence hidden in the long grass, the barbs spiking my knee. The Man snatched me up again and veered back towards the canal bank. I managed to shield my face with my arm so he was unable to clamp his hand over my mouth this time. I screamed and screamed and screamed.

When we reached the trees he stopped and dumped me onto the grassy bank, still trying to silence me. I continued to struggle and scream as he dragged me towards the canal. I couldn't swim. I knew he was going to push my head under those murky waters. My face was inches from the edge when I felt the pounding of feet on the earth under my belly before the sound reached my ears. The Man melted away as a young fellow burst from the towpath, yelling. He stopped momentarily to pull me to my feet before sprinting after my attacker. The young man's girlfriend came running along the path moments later and gripped my hand. The Man disappeared among the trees.

Although they seemed like adults to me at the time, my rescuers were only teenagers. They walked me home, the girl offering me Oddfellow sweets. If I close my eyes, I can still taste their spicy cinnamon and strawberry flavour. I remember that I didn't want my mother to know what had happened. I didn't want to get into trouble, so waved the young couple off at my front gate, saying I was okay. I was only home a few minutes when they returned, having second thoughts about leaving me there without telling anyone. My mother was cooking dinner, but after the couple left, she dropped everything to give me a bath. I protested. I was hungry. I had a bath the night before, with my sister. We didn't have a bath every night and in a big family like ours it was unusual to have a bathtub full of hot bubbly water just for one - and unusual for my mother to help me off with my dress and undies. Only with hindsight did I realise she was taking the opportunity to closely examine me and reassure herself that the only injury I had was a bloodied knee from the barbed wire.

I don't recall having any adverse effects from my encounter, apart from a small scar under my knee. I never saw The Man again although I continued to play along the canal banks and in the field, until the housing estate was extended and the field disappeared entirely. I have no memory of his face, which was shadowed by a cloth cap. His clothes were nondescript; dark trousers and jacket common to many older working men. Although a nine-year-old has only a limited understanding of sexual assault, at the time I knew that's why The Man grabbed me. But my biggest fear was of drowning in the canal. My relief at escaping drowning was greater than any fear of assault.

Eight years later, a close friend of mine was abducted in a car, driven to different locations and repeatedly raped when she was fifteen years old. At the time she described her night of terror in detail to me, but once the police business and medical examinations were completed, she put it behind her and we didn't speak of it again. Later, when I migrated to Australia we kept in touch over the years, writing long letters to each other, but we didn't meet again in person for twelve years. After a happy reunion, and several glasses of wine, she mentioned the sexual assault and told me her attacker was arrested and imprisoned about five years after the abduction. She had to testify in court when she was about six months pregnant with her first child and had to relive the fear and humiliation. I would never have raised the topic with her, but since she had raised it herself, I asked her what long-term effect it had had on her.

She mulled over my question for a few moments before answering me.

"The worst thing was that he pulled me from the car and raped me by the river that last time. I could smell the water and hear it flowing. I was terrified he would kill me by drowning me afterwards. But he drove me home in the middle of the night, threatening me all the time not to tell anyone. When we arrived, I could see my parents through the window, lights on, waiting up for me and I had this great surge of relief that I was still alive. I was home, I had escaped and my mum and dad were there for me. I was so glad to have survived."

When the police finally caught up with her attacker who had fled to England, he had stabbed a man and committed other serious assaults, so he was given a substantial prison term. This also helped her to move on.

Is there a woman alive who has not been subject to sexual harassment or sexual assault? I think not.

It has been over sixty years since The Man grabbed me and although I have rarely thought about it, I can recall the encounter with perfect clarity. I remember two other occasions as a teenager where I narrowly escaped being gang raped. My own daughter had a narrow escape as a ten-year-old and after a visit to the police station, I took her home, filled the bath and helped her off with her clothes as my own mother did with me, to reassure myself that she was unharmed.

Every woman experiences unwanted sexual advances. We all have stories about The Man on the bus, or in the theatre rubbing against you or touching your thighs. The guy at work, perhaps the boss, who stands too close to you, squeezes past you, or 'accidentally' touches your breasts.

Sometimes it's closer to home. The brother-in-law who thinks his wife's sisters are fair game. Or the ultimate betrayal; the father who rapes his daughter. One of the worst cases in recent times was dubbed the "Evil 8", where a father not only violently raped his ten-year-old daughter, but offered her up for sex to eight other men while he either watched or participated in the abuse.

As we navigate our way through life, sexual harassment is pervasive. From numerous, minor, unwanted sexual advances, to the life-changing effects of serious sexual assault. Although we have all experienced this to varying degrees, we were still shocked by the revelations of the #Me Too movement.

We were also shocked by the findings of the Royal Commission into Institutional Responses to Child Sexual Abuse. Not only by the extent of child sexual abuse by clergy, particularly in the Catholic Church, but by the extent of the cover-up. It is staggering how many voices have been successfully silenced over the years by the male hierarchy in so many religious organisations. Recently I watched the Four Corners program, *Bearing Witness: Exposing the secretive world of the Jehovah's Witnesses*. Girls reporting sexual abuse were interviewed by two male elders of the church to gauge the truth of their allegations. *The abuse had to be verified by two witnesses.* Fat chance! The mother and daughter interviewed in the program had been expelled and shunned by their church, cutting them off from family and friends, catapulting them from a close-knit, somewhat cloistered world to a friendless alien environment.

There have also been disturbing allegations of sexual harassment and sexual assault involving women working at Western Australian FIFO work sites.

Australian of the Year, Grace Tame, was repeatedly raped by her 58-year-old maths teacher, Nicolaas Bester, when she was fifteen. The twice convicted paedophile later bragged about the abuse online and in 2017 was sympathetically interviewed by fake clinical psychologist, sex therapist and men's rights defender, Bettina Arndt. She displayed a photograph of Grace taken from Facebook on the You Tube video of the interview with Bester and accused Grace of engaging in "sexually provocative behaviour". She also referred to the possibility of talking to young girls "about behaving sensibly and not exploiting their seductive power to ruin the lives of men."

Grace was unable to refute anything the paedophile said due to an archaic Tasmanian law preventing sexual assault survivors from speaking publicly. After a protracted and expensive legal challenge, Grace was given an exemption to the gag by the Tasmanian Supreme Court. Her activism and tenacity inspired Brittany Higgins to speak out about an alleged sexual assault in March 2019 by a colleague at Parliament House. Since then, four more women have made allegations against the same man.

Social media and the twenty-four-hour news cycle have created the opportunity for more women to take part in a global conversation. Will things improve now that so many genies are out of the bottle?

The National Women's Safety Summit ended in disappointment after the government accepted only six of the twelve recommendations from Sex Discrimination Commissioner Kate Jenkins' Respect@Work Report. Critics argue that it has failed to address violence towards women.

So, don't hold your breath, sisters. The Man's shadow continues to loom large in our lives.

Maria Bonar

'The Man' was highly commended in the Bronze Quill Award for creative nonfiction in 2021.

Wild Donkeys

There's a herd of wild donkeys
on the road to Wyndham.
Pulling over, I park by the roadside.
Camera in hand, I quietly
step down from the Landcruiser.
The herd freezes.

I move slowly forward
eager to capture an image
of these gorgeous creatures
sweet kohl-rimmed eyes
mascara'd lashes,
foals at foot.

Almost within snapping distance
a raucous bellow rends the air.
The leader of the pack challenges
from the other side of the road.
The herd bolts in one direction
I bolt in the other.

Panting in the heat, I leap
into the safety of my vehicle.
Behind me,
the vigilant male donkey
stands in a billow of red dust.
He sees me off the premises.

Maria Bonar

Yesterday's Rain

We grew together in our milky youth
strong, intertwined
bloomed and seeded
our features melded in our offspring

time passed
growth stunted
tethering each other
drastic pruning required.

recovery was slow
missing essential parts
we laboured to grow independently
adapted to our solo stakes

our offspring flourished
in yesterday's rain
now three generations of
companion plants

the final farewell in September
we buried you in our plot
at Pinnaroo
husband, father, grandfather

I visit you
with the kangaroos and their joeys
leave a flower from my garden
the bloom from a cutting you gave me
many years ago.

Maria Bonar

A Witch called Witchetypoo

Witchety for short

Witchetypoo's feet are something else. I mean they are still feet, as in — there are two of them — and they do smell like feet — but ugh, what a sight! Witchety's toenails are ten inches long, rough and ragged, crammed into pinchy, pointy boots with thin rubber soles. At the tips of her boots are holes where her nails furrow and fight for breath.

Witches have a creed that forbids them to cut their toenails — ever. If Witchety was to cut her toenails she would be expelled from The Society of Witches and die of shame. The shame is real. Other witches have died this way, shrinking and shrivelling until 'poof!', they are no more.

Witchety's ankles are impressively knobbly – like a shovelful of amorous snails stuffed into a pair of stockings. She has to battle with all of her witchy might to heave her boots over them.

Today her toenails are complete agony, all twisted and murderous. It takes enormous effort to launch her broomstick, scraping the ground harder and harder, faster and faster, like an angry bull. Sparks are needed to initiate take-off. For that to happen, Witchety must use enough fierce foot friction.

Eventually, sparks shoot menacingly and her broom rises, leaving a sickly smell. Behind her, a trail of smouldering nails, with a touch of burnt rubber, hovers in the gloom. Witchety's cat Gizzard hurls himself on at the last second, making her broom unbalanced. It wobbles, causing Witchety to curse.

Fortunately, her cursing is witchy swearing, not an evil spell cast on Gizzard. She manages to descend safely in a field of turnips, yelping on landing, as another toenail snaps completely off.

Gizzard has been known to cause the broom to crash. Worse than that, he was once de-haired by a stray spark. From fluff to puff in an instant. Since then, any hint of a spark or a toenail causes Gizzard to dissolve into a trembling mess. Witchety must cast a good spell to cure his post-traumatic toenail disorder. She tries in vain to remember the correct spell-making ingredients, but fails. Her witchy incompetence turns Gizzard into a sheep, then a screwdriver, and finally, a chicken kebab.

Hunched over a bubbling cauldron, Witchety fumbles through her trusty spell book, *Recipes for Spell Success.*

'*Ah, I see … just one frog's leg and half a bat's bladder. Seven spider's legs … and not the one for luck I dropped in last time. Silly Witchetypoo!*'

A wonky, toothless, chasm of a grin stretches across Witchety's face. '*Here we go! Hokus pocus … magic focus … MEOW! By the aroma of a thousand cauldrons, I proclaim you have stopped trembling, Gizzard. My spell has worked!*'

With that, Witchety launches into a celebratory dance of the ten ragged toenails.

'*Look at you, Gizzard,*' shrieks Witchety with a sweaty swagger. *You're calm and steady as a rock.*'

'*Oh, Gizzard, you really are a rock.*'

Erica Bowman

Memories

Contemplating her mother's unwavering presence during her younger years, Rachael sighs wistfully. Her memories are slipping away and becoming more elusive, filling her with angst.

The years 1967 until 1970 had been the best of times, full of adventure, laughter and love. Then, without warning, everything had shattered, like a dinner plate hurled at a wall. The broken pieces became Rachael's new emotions. Some sharp, some crushed and others crudely glued back together, never quite the same. Thrown into an emotional abyss, Rachael clung to her memories like a treasured old teddy, loved and hugged until limp and futile.

She remembers her mother's delicate, proportional frame, tiny in body and stature, her style elegant Parisian chic with 1950's swing dresses that accentuated her delicate curves and tiny waist. Rachael is sad that she can remember her mother's brown eyes, but not the sound of her voice.

Memories can be elicited in the most unexpected of ways. The piercing pleasure of a sherbet lemon erupting on her tongue instantly reunites Rachael with her mother in the late 1960s – a weekly shopping trip to Woolworths in a bustling Plymouth high street. Just the two of them.

Inside the store, near the toys, trays of sweets would beckon seductively with an explosion of colour. Quick and adept at crawling under the counter, Rachael would furtively grab the dropped Barley Sugars, Raspberry Ruffles and her favourite

Sherbet Lemons. The undiluted pleasure at finding these glistening jewels felt so beautifully illicit. Her mother, amused at her daughter's pirating antics, always grinned broadly as Rachael emerged victorious from under the counter. She had come to recognise her mother's smile as approval that she could keep her treasures.

Her haul was hastily folded into her jumper and brazenly tipped into her mother's handbag, the counter assistant turning a blind eye, as she always did. After their shopping trip, they would play a game. Rachael had to guess which sweet her mother had hidden behind her back. Sometimes, this game went on for half an hour. Mother had endless patience. Rachael enjoyed winning almost as much as eating the sugary delights.

Tea was deliciously predictable: a fondant fancy and honey sandwich served by her mother at exactly 4 pm, washed down with a glass of Ribena. Mother would sit bolt upright, slowly slicing an apple into impossibly thin pieces, savouring them slowly and pleasurably, closing her eyes as though she was enjoying an exquisite banquet.

At six o'clock on school days, Rachael had permission to watch Dr Who. She had felt so grown up and naughty. It had scary monsters that would send Rachael shrieking and scrambling onto her mother's lap. It was inappropriate viewing; they both knew that. Yet what stuck with Rachael was the knowing smiles exchanged between them. Most of all, she delighted in her mother's hugs, warm and safe. Coming home.

At night, tenderly tucked up in bed, a gentle noise had become familiar and comforting. A kind of mechanical lullaby: clickety-clack. Clickety-clack. Ding! Nimble fingers elegantly bouncing off keys like an enthusiastic pianist, rhythmic clattering of letters typed furiously with passion and precision – important letters written to important people – always copied onto black carbon paper, the originals folded with origami-like precision and placed into envelopes; the copies on a separate pile.

Rachael would wake each morning to a neatly stacked pile of letters. She would lick and stick each postage stamp, placing them meticulously on the envelopes, as her mother had shown her.

She had always sensed her mother was different – creative and quite brilliant. She could also be erratically impulsive. Life was an adventure. Always exploring new places and people.

Life for an adult Rachael had been feeling so empty, eliciting questions that didn't have answers. *Why did you go? Where are you? How can I find you?* There were so many missing pieces.

Rachael needed to follow her heart. She craved something more tangible than fading memories. She needed love, the kind of love that soothed her seven-year-old self and should never have been snatched from her.

At twenty-two, Rachael went in search of her mother. It was a brief journey, culminating in a telephone call to a psychiatric hospital. Her mother had been admitted there on several occasions. Her family did not approve of Rachael's search. They were afraid and ignorant about mental illness; an unhelpful combination that fed their prejudiced minds.

The hospital receptionist took Rachael's mother's name and started searching for it. Meanwhile, Rachael clung to her phone, eagerly and nervously, her heart pounding like a jackhammer. Was this going to be where she would find her mother and fill in the missing pieces? Would she still look effortlessly chic with wavy red hair and a signature brooch on her lapel? Would her mother still love her or want her?

The receptionist finally came off hold. 'I've found your mother's name.'

Rachael's heart pumped with joy.

Then she added: 'It's written in red.'

'What does that mean?' Rachael enquired.

Clearing her throat, the receptionist stated, 'I'm afraid it means the patient is deceased.'

'My mother has died?' Rachael's voice quivered.

'Yes, I'm so sorry.'

'Oh,' was all Rachael managed to gasp, before folding into a ball of pain that surged through every inch of her body. Her emotions followed with unforgiving rawness.

Two months later, Rachael is visiting a dilapidated, sprawling institution and is directed to a psychiatrist's dingy, depressing office. The busy floral wallpaper has seen better days and even better secrets. The office table is hidden from view under pots of pens, random stationery, assorted notes, and patient files that have spilled onto the floor like an erupting volcano. Rachael has never been in a psychiatrist's office before, but isn't perturbed at the disarray around her.

Mrs Edwards, the psychiatrist, a friendly, plumpish lady, has an unhurried air. Her crumpled clothes are dated and her feet firmly plant on the ground like an oak tree. She is pleasingly obliging and forthcoming. Rachael soon learns that she and her mother have similarities that could only be explained by genes. They had both studied art and were gifted writers. They loved to trawl second-hand shops, flea markets and have impressive collections of costume jewellery.

Rachael learns that her mother had a diagnosis of bipolar illness. This comes as a relief, as it explained not only her absences, but her adventurous personality with its impulsivity and sense of mischievousness. One big revelation is that her mother had applied for full custody of Rachael before her death. The stress involved had triggered a bipolar relapse, leading to another long psychiatric admission.

After a lot of searching and red tape, Rachael finally manages to track down her mother's meagre belongings: a box of costume jewellery, as eclectic, random and unique as her own; a carrier bag containing carbon copies of letters last seen on her mother's kitchen table. The letters feel enlightening and comforting, painful and happy, containing every facet of her mother's complex nature. Nothing has any monetary value. Rachael doesn't care. She has found most of the missing pieces and built an emotional bridge, reconnecting herself to her mother. Most importantly, she knows she was loved.

Erica Bowman

I Am

Reflections on Rottnest Cemetery.

They came, back then, in 1853,
foreheads frowned, heavy tread -
scuffed, scraped my crinkled skin
dug deep into my womb.
Sprinkled Holy Water,
chanted their strange tongue.
Buried him, Luke Ankerman.

They stood awhile. Pronounced me hallowed ground.

Could not they hear the music deep within
that which they were trampling?
My heart, deeply embedded in their grasp, pulsated
a sacredness, mine by right,
bestowed on me by a timeless divinity.

For eons past I've lived and breathed,
writhed, groaned, given birth.
I AM! The Holy One, Mother Earth.

Sun blessed, rain bathed, wind caressed.
In love and harmony, formed this land,
wove a timeless tapestry.
My swollen girth raised up high

mountains, hills, glens and dales.
My breasts oozed water of life,
baptised, consecrated living spirit.

They came again. Thirteen times they came again
to this wee patch they disdainfully claimed
the only place of hallowed ground.
Disregarded my eternal gift: resurrection.

The last time they came,
they gave me you, Patrick William O'Donaghue.

Shackled minds inhibit their capacity
to understand the ongoing mystery beneath their feet,
prevent them from knowing
'twas my dust from which you came,
my tender hand that pushed you forth.
For such a little time, ten short weeks.
Welcome home.

All eventually return to me.
I purge, cleanse and then release
unfettered spirit, breath and hope.
In my heaving bosom, a safe haven, you shall lie
a little while. Wait patiently, you'll soon be free.
You are not alone. Rest assured, I AM, I AM!

Have always been hallowed ground.

Elizabeth Brennan

Divine Intervention

Hi, my name's Dennis. Dionysus actually. Dionysus Backus. But my mates can't get their tongues around that. 'Specially when they're pissed, which they are most of the time. So everybody calls me Dennis. I don't mind. Been called a lot of things in my times, hey.

Got a lot of ribbing about my poofy name when I first arrived, till I showed off my sculling skills. Soon had them all trying to beat me, so was in with the mob okay once I drank them all under the table.

Just doin' my job, hey! Promoting booze. Always been good at it so, while I'm here, I thought I might as well cash in on my talent, so I'm getting a good screw from the Hotel's Association, for doing what I love. Really do enjoy my work.

Well, it wasn't hard getting these Aussie guys into the swing of it. Sales of beer went through the roof that first year.

But I do have another responsibility as God of Wine. Y'see, I love any old booze, but my first love is the lovely juice of the grape! That's the real thing! Not much available here, in those days though.

A few people were growing grapes and they seemed to thrive here, but only a few were making wine. It wasn't at all popular with my mates. 'Only women drink plonk,' I was told. 'Apart from Eye-talians and Greeks'.

Well, we Greeks think very highly of the noble grape, so I was somewhat affronted! Specially considering my own involvement in the development of the industry worldwide. So

I set out to change the situation.

It wasn't all that hard. These Aussies really love their booze. It was just a matter of breaking down those old prejudices, so I decided to concentrate on the sheilas. Women hadn't been welcome in the old-time pubs, so never really developed a taste for beer. And, though they wouldn't have admitted it, most of the better-off sheilas were snobs.

All I needed to do was slip a word in here and there in the right quarters, you know, reviews of posh restaurants, waffle about travel and the sophisticated drinking habits of us Europeans (Ha, Ha!), and they were ready to suck up any old kind of plonk.

Of course, once the hoi-polloi started getting into it, it was time to push the more expensive imports like champagne, so the snobs could believe their sophisticated 'noses' could really tell the difference.

When people started paying big money for imported plonk, the locals rushed to plant grapes – acres and acres of them. Now we have a real Aussie wine industry. It's booming, and drinking wine's become the favoured pastime of the upwardly-mobile Aussie.

That was my real triumph, hey. It's bloody good stuff too. I know. I've sampled all of it. And given it my approval. And you can't get a higher authority than the God of Wine.

Lynne Cairns

History

The past is a muddied tapestry
Soiled by toil and misery
Stained with pain and treachery
And the blood of guiltless men

But beneath the murk is a strong foundation
Eternal patterns of procreation
Weaving through each generation
Renewing life and hope again

For underneath the grime of time
And the built-up filth of sin and crime
Glimmering through dark avarice
Shine strands of love and sacrifice

So those who seek can find delight
In the human race's endless fight
Against the creed of might is right
That feeds on greed and exploitation

And the simple joys we share of right
The vibrant blues of peaceful night
The green of fields, and new-turned earth
Red as the blameless blood of birth

Search a little and you will find
Many a sign they've left behind
To help us understand our kind
And see their lives as inspiration

Lynne Cairns

Just Get Off the Train

It would be so easy
To just get off the train
Walk up that little street
And disappear

To leave behind the worries
The burdens that I bear
The other people's traumas
That weigh heavy on my mind

Could I leave them all behind
Like some abandoned load of terror?
To be tracked down by Security
And disarmed

Maybe I could ring them
And warn them to beware
Not to be infected
With my cares

Then I'd find a cheap motel
And book myself a room
And ring home
When I knew no one was there

To say that I'm OK
I just had to go away
Don't you worry and don't bother the Police
I'll be back when I have found out who I am

Lynne Cairns

Lost in Time

06.00 am

I love this time of the morning. It's so peaceful out here. If I try, the traffic noise on the Freeway can sound like the sea in the distance, so it's just me and the birds, and the early morning breeze.

I like to get up an hour early, just to get in this time of peace and quiet. That's when I feel really creative. I've even started dreaming of writing a novel. Managed to get some of it on paper this morning.

See, I've got this great idea. There's this woman who's so weighed down with responsibilities. You know, husband and kids always after her at home, and a nagging boss at work who's never satisfied. It all kind of builds up in her, but she tries to keep everybody happy, even though she sometimes feels as if she's losing her mind.

Oh! There's the alarm. I'd better go and stir him up before he turns it off and goes back to sleep. It's my day off today and I told him and the kids they'd have to get themselves ready because I'd be trying to work out here in the patio.

Now, where was I! Oh! Yes. One day, on her way in to work after a fight with her husband, the thought of facing another barrage of complaints from the boss is just too much, and she just flips! When the train stops at one of the old suburban stations, she just gets off, walks up the hill, and vanishes. Feel like that myself some mornings.

Gee! Seven fifteen! If I don't hear any movement soon, I'd better go and

Getting back to this woman, she'd often wondered what it would be like to walk into another house and be someone else, and that's what happens. Suddenly she's somewhere else. In another time. And she has a new life there. Could be interesting. If I ever get the chance to write it.

Oh! Good! Joe's up – yelling at the kids to be quiet because Mummy's trying to work out the back. He is a dear really. "What's that? No! I don't know where your socks are. Try the sock drawer!"

I haven't decided where I'll put her yet. I was thinking maybe Celtic Britain, or Regency England, though I guess those times have been a bit overdone, what with King Arthur and all the Jane Austen stuff. Old-time Australia might be better. Maybe around here somewhere, so she could live in a house that's still there. It could be during the Great Depression or World War II.

*There they go again – "Mum! Mum! **Mum!**" Why don't you call your bum Mum. Then you'll always have it with you! That's what my old Dad used to say. Poor old Dad. I wish he was still here. I miss him a lot. Mum seems to be coping, but she seems so lonely at times*

A postman on a pushbike tips his hat as he rides past blowing his whistle each time he pops mail into a letterbox. She's surprised how many women are at home and can spare the time to come out to chat to the mailman or their neighbours.

"Can someone please let the dog out?"

None of the houses have garages or carports, but all have big backyards with chicken pens, fruit trees and vegie gardens. None of that seems strange to her, though, because everything fits with the new memories flooding her mind. She knows exactly where she is and where she's going. Number thirty-nine, with the big peppermint tree out the front. I can see her lifting the latch on the gate and walking around to the back door. Inside, she heads for the bedroom to take off the hat that wasn't on her head when she left home, kicks off her worn best heels and carefully removes her heavily darned stockings.

"Your gym boots? On the front porch!" (I couldn't stand the smell!)

Maybe her husband's away fighting or working for the dole somewhere. The dole wasn't much, and in those days there just weren't many jobs for women. Wonder how many kids she's got. Maybe a man calls selling rabbits or trying to sell her something she would love but can't afford, like a vacuum cleaner. Maybe he's rather cute and they have an affair. Things could get really bad if hubby comes home and finds out. Men could get pretty frustrated and angry not being able to support their families. Does he drink? Get violent?

"What piece of paper? When did you have it last? - You left it on the table last week? Do you really expect it to still be there! It's it in your pocket? Oh good."

I'll need to decide what happens to her. There are such a lot of possibilities. I think, though, that she would maybe have occasional glimpses of her old life. Possibly in dreams that become increasingly intrusive, and she starts to worry about those kids she had back then, in the future; and her poor old Mum. She thinks her other hubby will be OK. All her girlfriends thought he was a gem, so some woman is sure to have latched onto him, but then the kids would have a step-mum, and step-mums have a bad name, thanks to all the fairy tales.

"You're going? OK love. Kiss kiss! Have a good day. Don't let the bastards wear you down!"

So I guess I'd have to bring her back, of course. Some sort of resolution. Yeah, how to end it, that's a big problem. Happy endings are nice but not seen as real literature. All the real literature seems to end miserably.

It's very quiet in there! Hope everything's alright.

Perhaps time has stood still, but if not, Hubby will have found someone else, the kids turned into teenagers, and her Mum's probably dead. Or maybe, the world's been destroyed by nuclear warfare or global warming. No that's just too depressing to think about.

Oh hell! Sounds like they're murdering each other.

"What on earth is going on? Jamie, get down from there! Taylor, stop strangling Krystal this minute. Careful Jamie, you'll tip it over. Noooo!"

01.30pm - Well, thank God, Jamie's shoulder was only dislocated. Gave him a scare and it hurt when they popped it back, so I guess he might think twice before climbing up the bookcase again. He got really upset and they gave him a sedative. He's sleeping now, so I'm back here trying to get my brain working again. Thought I was on a roll this morning, but it all seems to have slipped away. Oh well, I'll get myself a coffee. Or maybe something stronger.

Lynne Cairns

Love

Love is a cruel and sneaky thing
that creeps up unexpectedly
and strikes us with impunity
without a word of warning

If due to false security
you think you have immunity
you may find that you are wrong
some fateful day or morning

The chances are a stranger's glance
or something new in an old friend's smile
sends you stumbling distractedly
off the fragile edge of sanity

As you wander far from reality
you never know you've been ambushed
until you fall - or were you pushed
by love?

Lynne Cairns

Northam

It's nice to see you looking well, old town
When so many of your mates have dwindled down
To sad, forlorn, forgotten places
Full of empty shops and lonely faces

You're still prepared to welcome travellers in
Old buildings glow with paint and on each bin
You tell your story without affectation
With scattered sculptures adding punctuation

Lynne Cairns

The Burning

I stand and watch the building burn, the red glare glittering through my tears. Tortured glass explodes, as broken, blackened beams crash to the ground. The cleansing fire consumes it all. Soon nothing is left but the fading scent of shattered dreams, and the bitter echoes of a love that turned to hate.

Nothing remains of the life we lived. No charred and twisted shoes or broken toys, only the memories of bitter hurt. Nothing's there to show you ever lived; that I was ever here. Only glowing ashes and the oily, choking smoke. No fingerprints, no blood, no DNA.

Lynne Cairns

The Haunted House

The rain hammered on the old tin roof, cascading over the verandah as the water overflowing from the water tank dug a deep ditch beside the stone foundations. No one lived there since old Mr Blake was found dead in the kitchen three years ago. Even before that, people said it was haunted. No one seemed to remember why.

Sitting safe above the flood line, the old place had laughed at storms and floods for a hundred-and-fifty years. But the river was rising and this was no ordinary flood. Upriver, torrential rain broke the decade-long drought and washed away everything in its path.

It was a hectic time for the rescue teams, busy saving lives. So it was not until all had been accounted for, that anyone noticed the big pine tree behind the house had crashed to the ground, its tangled roots taking with them half the back verandah and sleepout and leaving a deep hole filled with water and debris.

When the worst of the emergency was over and the floodwater began to subside, neighbours became worried that the deep, mud-filled cavity might be a danger to children or straying livestock. So council inspector Sarah Jones was sent to assess the risk.

Sarah, who grew up in the area, shrugged off the chills prickling her forearms as she approached the derelict building, attributing her illogical fear to the stories of skeletons in the cellar her schoolmates used to scare each other with.

Until she saw the bones, that is, and remembered a talkative old neighbour telling her dad, 'No one believed Charlie Blake's mother ran off with a travelling salesman. The old folk reckoned Charlie's old man done her in.'

Hoping what she was seeing were old bones, Sarah snatched her phone from her pocket and called the local police. Within minutes several police cars arrived. After a brief interview, Sarah headed back to work as the forensic team got to work.

It was two days before a brief report appeared in the papers. There were two skeletons, one female, one male, that were believed to have been there for over seventy years. Is that what became of Mrs Blake and her travelling salesman?

Lynne Cairns

The Luck of the Irish

It was only October in Ireland, but already the ancient laneway was carpeted with rustling red and gold leaves, as Terry and Caitlin wandered between high banks topped by tangled brambles and the holly bushes that would brighten the scene when all else faded to monotone greys and the white of snow.

'Look Caitie,' cried Terry, 'There's still one pear on the old pear tree. I wonder if it's still OK to eat. I'm going to climb up and get it.'

'Be careful Terry,' his sister told him. 'You don't want to break your leg or something just in time for the holidays.'

Carefully, the redheaded boy clambered up the twisted old tree trunk and reached out to grasp the last pear of summer, but the branch he was clinging to creaked, then cracked, and came crashing down, tossing Terry into a tangled briar rosebush.

'Owwwww!' he shrieked.

But was that another, higher-pitched voice echoing his cry?

'Ow, Owwooo! Get off me ye great galumphing spalpeen. Get off of me!'

Trying to avoid getting caught on any more horrible thorns, Terry painfully pulled himself up to sit on the bank and turn to see who was yelling at him. There was a rustling in the grass under the briar and a wild, red-bearded face appeared, followed by a small green-clad body.

'Get ye gone, ye blitherin' great craiture. Get ye gone!'

'No, I won't,' whispered Terry, who knew immediately what to do in such a situation. Clutching the wee man by one leg, the boy dragged him out of his hiding place.

'Now, I've got you,' he crowed, 'and you must take me to your pot of gold.'

'Ah, me boyo,' came the plaintive reply. 'Ye've come too late. We leprechauns used to have great pots of gold, but the big people came and made us an offer we couldn't refuse. They took all the gold in exchange for one billion American dollars in bitcoin.'

Lynne Cairns

The Rains Came

The rain finally came, hammering on the iron roof, though we'd wondered if the long drought would ever end. If the poor cracked soil could ever soften and allow the sleeping seeds to stir.

The insects knew it was coming. Ants had been moving house, carrying their precious progeny to higher ground and raising the earth mounds to direct the flood away from the chambered columns of their homes. Scorpions scurried and centipedes skittered on their multiple feet, seeking dryer premises.

Like the frogs in the creek croaking in delight, we danced in the rain and cheered, as tiny rivulets flowed across the thirsty soil. Swirling around rocks and fallen branches, they joined together to fill the creeks. When they overflowed, we moved the stock to higher ground.

And still it rained. The waters poured across roads, swallowing our crops, washing away trees, sheds and fences. We watched as it rose higher, drowning the orchard and garden, before creeping in under the locked door, climbing to the windows to cascade down inside. When it reached waist-high, we climbed on the roof

And here we sit, shivering as our poor drowned sheep sweep by. We hear the heart-rending mooing of the few cattle still standing belly-deep on the hilltop. That high ground wasn't high enough, it seems. A tree whirls by with a snake entangled in its top branches. A kangaroo clinging to a torn-off branch loses its battle as we watch.

We hear a helicopter, but it turns away to the south. As its thumping fades, there's just the swishing of water, the bumping and grinding of heavy debris, the creaking of the old house and the squeaky song of the old windmill

It's ridiculous, I know, but that sound had been a strangely comforting reminder that generations had survived out here, and so would we. But now the song ends in a harsh shriek as a tree crashes into the mill, before swirling away in the flood. In the lurid red glow of sunset, I see the mast leaning at a precarious angle. I'll have to do something about that in the morning, if it's still there.

If I'm still here.

Lynne Cairns

By George!

A letter, lying in the old rusting letterbox, looked official. Sandy didn't like official-looking envelopes, so her hand trembled slightly as she reached in to pull the brown envelope from the box. Underneath this first letter, she could see two other letters: another envelope that also looked suspiciously official, but the third one was a more delicate, creamy white envelope. *Three letters in the box on one day has to be an omen, but not a good one*, thought Sandy, wrinkling her nose. Her grey eyes squinted under furrowed brows.

She stood for a few more moments looking at the envelopes, which tingled the fingertips of her right hand. As she closed the rusty mailbox, Sandy looked up to see if neighbours in the street were watching: *They do watch everyone and everything that happens in the street.* And, as most of the neighbours used the internet for email, Sandy's postie-delivered mail was something of a novelty, to be observed and commented on at the supermarket or over the fence.

'They'll want to know every detail about my mail next week,' Sandy told the recently delivered mail. Clutching the envelopes tightly, with a little triumphant wave of three envelopes in the air, she turned sharply and returned through the safety of her front door. The image of her name on three envelopes was imprinted on her eyes—*Ms S Rey, 3 South Bay Road, Smytton*. It really was something to get three letters on the same day, when most days the box was empty—but Sandy checked for the mail every morning, just in case.

Her small frame disappeared into the shadows of the house, where she'd lived alone these past thirty years. While she appeared vulnerable, almost frail, Sandy had been an athlete in her youth, and maintained her fitness into the latter part of what she called her *middle ages*, but she was a shy person for all her physical strength and strong will. These days, she noticed that she couldn't walk so far and fast, and aches in her knees and hips were more frequent. Not one to complain, Sandy merely observed these changes in her body with curiosity.

Three envelopes! Now there's something, thought Sandy, as she turned the envelopes over in her hands, looking for some clue to the senders. One envelope was dated two months ago. *Where had that one been?* wondered Sandy. *Not yet,* she paused, *time for a cuppa before I open these.*

'Three is not always a coincidence,' she observed aloud as she sat with a steaming cup of coffee at the kitchen table. She pursed her lips, looking first at the small pile of letters. Turning her eyes away, savouring the moment of anticipation, Sandy looked out the window into her garden to see the herbs, native shrubs and roses in profusion, all eagerly visited by a miscellany of small birds and insects.

'There's the Trinity,' Sandy recalled from her long past membership of a church. 'And death seems to come in threes. Yet sometimes three can be the start of something: *Ready, Set, Go!* Not always an end,' Sandy explained to the birds flitting around in her garden, remembering her days as an athlete on the starting blocks.

She put the long, brown envelope to one side, knowing it was from the clinic on the mainland. She recognised the address printed on the front — ABC Wellness. ABC always brought a sly smile to her lips as she recalled the acronym from her travelling days. "Not another ABC"—Another b****y castle— was the travellers' cry whenever a tour bus stopped at the next historical site. In her present situation, *clinic* was the operative word.

The other two letters intrigued her, particularly the creamy white, textured envelope. The return address was Hopetoun on the mainland. It didn't ring a bell. The second and smaller official envelope bore an embossed crest of some government department. She didn't recognise the name of the Department of Community and Civics. *Probably a fine for shouting at Mrs Hillbilly (or whatever her name is) about her barking dog. I definitely was not civil that day.* Sandy put that letter aside to sit with its brown companion next to the toaster on the kitchen counter.

The cup of coffee became cold dregs. Sandy could no longer postpone opening the third letter. She thought it a pity to tear the high-quality paper with her improvised letter opener. As she unfolded the contents, a small photo fell out onto the table. Turning it over, Sandy could see it was a photo of a small boy about three to four years old. He looked familiar, but she couldn't think whose child he might be. Sandy had no children, no immediate family, nor friends with children this age. She narrowed her eyes, studying the details of the boy's smiling face.

'It's George!' The sound of her exclamation startled her, as she recognised the small boy from that ferry crossing last winter. 'By George, it's George!' she reprised. A smile softened her voice, hazing her eyes. The picture blurred momentarily until she wiped away the tears with the corner of her t-shirt.

As she opened her eyes slowly, Sandy was no longer in her kitchen. She could smell the ozone of the ocean; feel the movement of a ship. She was on the ferry again, crossing the rough passage between her island home and the mainland. *Must be over six months. I almost forgot,* she thought, pulling an invisible rug around her shoulders and settling into a deckchair.

The ship rose and fell with the rhythm of the ocean. The blue sea turned green-grey. The wind changed direction, whipping up white caps. Sandy huddled on the lee side of the ship, on a sheltered section of the deck. She was hoping against hope that the wind would drop with the sunset for she was starting to feel very uncomfortable sitting hunched in the deckchair, the ship's monogrammed rug tight around her shoulders — a shield against the rising sea spray. A shiver ran through her. Her stomach protested and her head felt heavy. *Is this just sea sickness?* she wondered. Watching the horizon, Sandy let her body roll with the motion of the ship to synchronise eyes and ears: an effort to control this rising mal de mer, if that's what she was feeling. The sky was grey and darkening. The ocean surrounded the ship with white-lipped ridges and crests of the battering waves. The wind-borne spray left a light wet sting on her face.

As the chill spread through her, Sandy stood and, still wrapped tightly in her ship's blanket, cautiously made her way to the forward section, to the Carousel Bar, situated just under the bridge, overlooking the ship's bow. Even though this is one part of a ship that experiences the maximum rise and fall of the waves, it held some comfort. Davy, the bartender in this out-of-the-way ship's bar, was very sympathetic, knowing that champagne was a good balm for sea sickness; well, at least it dulled the senses in a pleasant way. *And*, Sandy noted, *the sun is over the yardarm!*

With her back to any other travellers, Sandy found a table near one of the small rectangular portholes. The bar was almost empty as most passengers seemed to prefer the ferry's larger, noisier social hubs. After the first glass of bubbling champagne, Sandy sat back, gazed out over the bow, beyond which she could see the white caps still rising. The ship dipped, then reared as it cut its way through the rising, darkening sea, sending spray high over the bow. Sandy focused on the champagne glass as if it held powers of prophesy of a crystal ball. Her mind wandered around the reason for her voyage. No prophesies emerged from the miniature ocean turbulence in the champagne flute. Yet, there was something calming, watching the prow of the ship slice into the waves. Sandy settled into the distraction of its rhythm, to be entertained as she anticipated the next wave—*Would its spray go higher and further across the bow and deck than the previous wave?*

It was only a short distance, but often a slow crossing between the island and the mainland, for the currents made this crossing particularly rough with the right combination of wind and tide conditions. It was a crossing she didn't want to make for more than one reason. Not yet anyway. But she had appointments with medical specialists about a health concern that she had ignored for some time. She had always been fit for her age. Nothing serious, she told herself, just a twinge, until the twinge became an ache, and the ache became a pain! It was time to face reality; time to contemplate all the possibilities.

Sandy hadn't searched any of those medical sites on the Internet, knowing her hypochondriacal tendencies would take over; that in her self-diagnosis, imagining every malady known to medicine. Such imaginings could take on dark shapes in her mind. Her heart would pound, her breath a gasp as her chest tightened, until she was able to push the anxieties back into their hiding place. So, she sipped the champagne, letting the bubbles tickle her nose, as she reassured herself that she had made the right decision. She relaxed as the nauseous sensations also eased.

Feeling better, Sandy noted that the wind had dropped. The champagne seemed to have a calming effect on the wind and ocean, too. After folding her rug, she left the bar to venture out on deck, thinking about decisions she might have to make. *Not yet out of the frying pan and into the fire, but that may be one outcome*, she mused, then chastened herself. *Ah! I'm so full of clichés.* Stopping to lean on the railing, pushing those negative thoughts away, she reviewed what she needed to do even if the prognosis was not serious or terminal. Whatever the outcome, she would still have to put her "affairs in order" as her friends urged her. *Prepare for my death, that's what they meant,* she thought.

At those recollections, Sandy dropped back to the warm comfort of her kitchen with a jolt, shook her head and wiped her eyes. *That was weird,* she thought. *I've never felt like that before. Perhaps that's what Shirley MacLaine felt when she had her out-of-body experiences! Maybe life doesn't end, maybe we just slip inside ourselves where our memories and experiences survive…* Sandy looked around the kitchen, slowly orienting herself. Not yet out of the patchwork of past memories, she lingered on some of thoughts and concerns…

Who would know the family's stories behind their treasures that all now resided with her? There was nobody who could be a custodian for those items that held such precious memories. No siblings. No children. No one knew that the silver spoon, dated 1803, was her present to her parents for their 25th wedding anniversary, or the story of the knobkerrie that her grandmother, when a girl, brought back from Africa, or that the grey Noritake fine china cup, saucer and plate set belonged to her grandfather, nor his stories of his life in America in 1911. Their faces surrounded her, smiling, as she conjured them from past familial settings. *There's so much to do to prepare for one's death.* Sandy closed her eyes, drifting into her reverie as the image of George drew her back to the ferry crossing.

A heavy ocean spray was cold as she leaned back in her deckchair. She realised that she had been so self-absorbed with her own concerns and fears for several months that she had lost touch with events around her. She couldn't remember the last time she read a newspaper, watched the news on television or accepted any invitations from friends. She suddenly felt guilty about neglecting those closest to her. She stood unsteadily gripping the railing as the ship's slow roll inserted itself under her feet, and the light-headedness from the champagne joined forces. Sandy watched a lone seagull swoop into, then rise above the mist that trailed in the ship's wake. *Ups and downs, just like life,* Sandy huffed to herself.

As all these thoughts roamed around her mind, her eye caught a flash of colour to her right. Red, she registered. The colour of danger raised an alarm in her mind and body. She turned around, looking in the direction of the colour flash to see a small boy of about three years old, running as fast as only a small child can. He was heading towards the aft-deck of the ship. The deck was slippery from the spray that earlier washed over the rail. *Where's the child's mother?* Sandy thought as she looked around the deck. *Should I do something?* she asked herself, unsure of intervening. Seeing no one, Sandy started to hurry in the direction the child had taken. She staggered slightly with the roll of the ship. 'Ooops!' she said out loud to herself.

The child was easy to see in his red jacket—a beacon in the fading light. He was still moving away from her. She clutched at the rail along the cabin wall as the ferry rolled again. She righted herself and started to run, feet finding air, then the deck again. Behind her came a loud cry funnelled by the wind along the deck.

'George! George! Stop! George!' The mother, too far away to catch George.

Sandy tried to run faster. The ship rolled to starboard as she rounded the cabin wall onto the afterdeck. There she came upon the child stopped momentarily by the open space of deck stretching out before him: an unhindered view of the churning ocean beyond the stern railing, trailing away to the horizon. Sandy slid to a stop, grabbing the child at the same time. As they collided, the momentum of the ship shuddering into the next wave knocked them to the deck. The duo slid towards the last railings of the stern. *We'll miss the taffrail!* The word suddenly formed in Sandy's mind as time stood still. *Where did that come from?* she wondered—a discordant thought given their situation.

If Sandy thought that her life had passed in front of her eyes before, the vision this time was in technicolour and at least 60 frames per second as she and the child slid on the wet deck. The child wriggled in her grip. Sandy drove her feet into the deck to try to stop the skid, but the pair slid onwards towards the misty void beyond the stern.

Sandy hit the stanchion side-on. The duo jerked to a sudden stop. They lay still, winded, the child limp in her arms. With a gasp, they were both breathing hard again. The wind dropped; the sea calmed; a moment of absolute stillness surrounded them. The wake of the ship spread out beyond the stern to the horizon. Sandy and George were held fast by the stanchion.

Hands grasped them; pulled them; lifted them. The child was no longer in her arms. Sandy sat up slowly, then stood up rather unsteadily, supported by two of the crew. She looked beyond the hands holding her, looking for George and his mother. The rescued and rescuers moved away from the edge of the stern to deck chairs in the shelter of the promenade deck.

'Thank you. Thank you,' sobbed the young mother, clutching little George to her. Sandy sat watching a young man in uniform, whom she presumed was the husband and father, holding them close.

'Oh, Bill, I will never let him out of sight again,' sobbed the young woman into her husband's chest, as they both embraced the small boy.

'George and the woman are both safe now, Kathrine,' comforted Bill, his deeper voice cracked with emotion. In the next breath, they were gone, ushered away. Sandy was supported by a couple of the crew members, who thanked her for her quick reaction and courage to make such an amazing rescue. Sandy, herself, was wondering how she had managed to move so quickly. Imaging what might have happened to the child, and to her. She shivered and shook, feeling hot and cold alternately. The crew dispersed after assisting Sandy below decks to the medical centre. She felt an overwhelming sense of emptiness, an aloneness.

Later that evening at dinner, Sandy looked for the young couple, hoping for a chance to talk with them, but she couldn't see them anywhere in the crowded dining room. After the rescue, Sandy and George did not cross paths at the medical centre, so there was no opportunity to talk with his parents or to see George again. *They've disappeared.* There was something familiar about the family, but she couldn't quite place where she might have seen them before. Her face set into her serious, pensive visage, brow bunched, eyes narrowed, lips pursed.

During that night, Sandy tossed uneasily to some bad dreams, reliving the "what-if" scenarios of the strange rescue on that strange yesterday. She had some colourful bruises taking shape on her hip and ribs from the hard contact with the taffrail stanchion to remind her that saving little George really had happened. For the remainder of the voyage, she continued to wonder who the young family could be but didn't see them around the ship or on disembarkation.

The sharp memories of the rescue faded with her bruises. Soon the incident rested in the back of her mind as she pursued her medical appointments, and multiple tests and scans in the city. Exhausted by the hustle and bustle of the big city, Sandy was relieved to return home to wait for the results of all the tests prescribed by her mainland doctors. The homeward bound crossing was so uneventful that Sandy almost hoped for another runaway child to break the monotony.

The letters! The letters! Remembering the letters waiting for her inspection, Sandy, again roused from her recollections and reveries to focus her attention on the three letters. Inside the white envelope, a card with a brief note accompanying the photo of young George. *Thank you for your kindness and courage in rescuing our precious George …* Skipping to the last words of the card's message, Sandy read — *We wish you the same joy and happiness. Kathrine and Bill.* Sandy sat stunned.

'By George! It wasn't them!' she said out loud, confused by her conjured, mistaken identity. She nodded, then smiled softly to herself, in response to the warmth of the expression of joy contained and delivered by the written words written in the delicate white card. Checking the date on the envelope, Sandy was again surprised that this piece of mail had taken six months to reach her.

Just then the doorbell rang. Next came a loud knocking. Sandy placed the half-read card on the table, standing, moving slowly to the front door, her mind occupied by the revelations of the card and its photo. Through the smoky glass, she could see two shapes. Hesitantly, she opened the door just a crack to see who was on her doorstep. The tall man in uniform smiled and spoke confidently. Sandy couldn't find the words to greet unexpected guests at her door.

'Good afternoon, Ms Rey? I am Commander William George Verlle, currently on secondment to the Governor's Office on special assignment to the Department of Community and Civics. We are contacting people who were involved in an incident on the mainland ferry last May. May I come in to discuss your recollection of the events of May 6?'

Sandy stood looking at the confident expression on the officer's face and noticed that his eyes conveyed a softer persona, but she hesitated to open the door.

'Yes, I'm Sandy Rey.'

Commander Verlle asked again. 'May we come in? It is important that I clarify the differences between the reports of the incident from other passengers. We need to talk privately about this matter.'

With no response from Sandy, the Commander continued, 'I understand that you chased a small boy on the ferry deck and that you grabbed him, falling to the deck. We have no interview or written reports from you to explain what happened. Some passengers' reports suggested that it could be a case of child abuse or assault. Therefore, it is important that we clarify this matter. May we discuss this inside?'

The Commander's words hit Sandy in the chest, like a punch from a world-class boxer. Her stomach clenched with nausea, her heart seemed to stop, and her head was floating off her shoulders. Her eyes popped open with shock and surprise.

'Oh, no! Err, yes!' Sandy widened the crack in the door, looking uncertainly at the uniformed stranger. With the wider view, she could see the smaller figure, also in uniform, standing just behind the tall Commander.

'Please, call me Bill. And let me introduce you to George, my son.' Commander Verlle smiled, as he reached around his left leg, taking George's hand to manoeuvre him to stand before the partly opened door.

Surprise took another dimension. Shock faded quickly. Tears welled in her eyes, and her voice deserted her. Sandy opened the door wide to welcome the uniformed visitors into her small house.

Over coffee, milk and homemade shortbread, Bill Verlle apologised if his words sounded like a harsh accusation. He explained that he put no credence in the assault claims, finding them baseless after reviewing the available reports. Her reaction and version of events confirmed his conclusions. The other purpose of his visit, he continued, was to find people who had been identified for courage and bravery during the past year, but who had not responded to an invitation to attend the Governor's presentation to acknowledge those recipients and their extraordinary deeds.

'As it took us some time to find you, and as the Governor's Office did not receive your reply, I sought special permission to contact you directly, given your special place in my family's life. If you accept the invitation, I also have special permission to escort you to Government House for the occasion.'

As his father spoke, little George grinned shyly at Sandy over his glass of milk. Sandy smiled back, taking in his wide blue eyes, smile, the colour of his hair, and his likeness to his father. Her previous uncertainty of the identity of the child she saved faded in the wonderful warm, live image of the little boy sitting at her table. Sandy complimented him on his smart uniform.

'Just like daddy's, 'cos I want to be a sailor, too.' His light baby voice, trying to sound so grown up, tugged at Sandy's heart.

Sandy accepted the invitation and, with Bill's guidance, made plans for her attendance at Government House in two months' time. She stood looking down the road long after the two sailors departed.

'You never know what will happen next!' Sandy muttered to no one in particular. Smiling, she thought, *this visit by an official government car and three letters all in one day will definitely entertain the local gossips for weeks to come!*

Back at her kitchen table, Sandy finished reading Kathrine's message advising her of the intended visit by Bill and George. Sandy smiled again at the photo of little George as the card and photo slipped back into their envelope. The long-delayed Governor's official invitation confirmed Bill's information. It was set aside with the George letter.

Turning over the ABC envelope, Sandy hesitated. Her face softened by a deep inner smile. *Three is not a coincidence!* With a firm grip, she slipped the old fruit knife under the edge of the flap of the third envelope.

Sue Colyer

Life After

I'm now managing to negotiate the single life since my husband Martin died in July 2019. Now that it's March 2023 I'm coming to terms with living alone. I discuss this with a friend as we sit Al Fresco in the courtyard of a coffee shop in Perth City Centre. We choose to eat in the fresh air as the threat of COVID-19 still lingers.

'You have friends, interests, and you look happy,' she says.

'It was traumatic at first, but it's a problem most women must, sooner or later, face,' I tell her.

At first, people rallied around; there was the funeral, and then so many details to sort out. I realise I was emotionally numb, and went through the motions of everyday living. Martin had always organised the finance and technical stuff as he ran a business while I looked after the domestic side. I organised social events, performed home duties, and looked after the welfare of our three children. I know that's old fashioned nowadays, but it worked as we had a loving compatible relationship which lasted for over sixty years. I went straight from the parental home to married life, so I'd always had people around me. Now, although my children help me with practical things like finance and shopping, they are busy living their own lives.

'So, I guess the main problem for single women is loneliness,' my friend says.

'It's not having one special person who cares, who is willing to share problems; someone who has a sense of humour, but above all it's the lack of physical contact.'

At home, I broke up the day by walking to the Park Van in the nearby-recreation centre. The owners have put up an awning; there are tables and chairs where lonely people sit drinking coffee and chatting to each other. After Martin's demise, one of the elderly men, whose dog accompanied him, suggested, 'Why don't you get a dog for company?'

'A dog wouldn't replace my husband; it would be a liability; I was brought up in a London apartment where we didn't have animals,' I said.

At first, I wanted to escape so visited my close friend who lives on the Sunshine Coast. She and her husband have been happily married for many years, which accentuated the fact I was alone, especially as we'd previously been a foursome. We all talked about Martin, and how we missed his presence. I even showed them the video of the funeral, and talked about his courageous suffering with Motor Neuron Disease.

My friend, who is squeamish, she said, 'Please stop talking about death; it's so depressing.' So I put on a happy face, and managed to enjoy the rest of the holiday.

When I returned to Perth, I browsed through the travel supplements. The vision of an exotic holiday in foreign parts lightened my despondent mood, but later the advent of the COVID pandemic destroyed my pipe dreams. Perth was in lockdown so I hardly saw anybody. I didn't even go to the supermarket, and had my food home delivered. Only one hour's walk a day, while wearing a mask, was permitted, so watching T.V. and reading was my main recreation. I should have passed my time writing stories but, feeling depressed, I lacked the incentive so I frittered the days away.

I looked for other diversions. Although I realised I could never replace my husband and had no desire to live with anyone else, I thought it would be pleasant to meet a male companion.

I would pay for myself when we went out, so there would be 'no strings attached.' I looked to some of my divorced and widowed friends for advice.

One had met a widower in his eighties at the Rotary club. They went on a cruise; he had old fashioned values so he proposed on the deck of the ship one starry night. She accepted, but said first they must get approval from their children. To do this, they must go to a lawyer and draw up a prenuptial agreement – otherwise, their offspring might feel threatened with losing their inheritance. But it must all have been too much for the widower because shortly after the holiday he dropped dead of a heart attack.

Another friend found a suitable man online, but she was ten years my junior. Yet another had a bad experience when she met a man who continued to stalk her after she rejected him. I didn't want the hassle, and besides, by this time, I was beginning to enjoy the positive aspects of single life. I began to appreciate the freedom to be independent; to eat, sleep, and come and go as I pleased.

Mature age men, even though half presentable, find themselves in the fortunate situation of being surrounded by unattached women. I live in a retirement village where there are twelve couples, sixty single women, and only fifteen men. I decided not to take the path of browsing the internet, as I might prove easy prey for predatory males who seek out emotionally vulnerable women. One man in the village appeared genuinely grieved when his wife died of pancreatic cancer. Females rallied round him, cooked him delicious food, and did their best to console him. Six months later I bumped into him at the village club house.

'How are you coping?' I asked.

'I have found a new lady.' He was all smiles. 'My wife and I knew her many years ago, and she showed up at the funeral.

Only drawback is she lives a distance away.'

'Well, you can always have sleepovers,' I said.

'Don't worry … we have plenty of those,' he said.

I don't begrudge him his pleasure as women live longer than men, so I suppose in that respect we are the ultimate winners.

There are days, I confess, when I wallow in self-pity, but really, my default mood is a cheerful attitude to life. So far, I'm healthy and active, my three children, who are decent human beings, have chosen charming partners who possess integrity. I have four grandchildren and three great-grandchildren. As in most families, there are problems, so I wish Martin was here to lighten the load; but I know he would be pleased that I'm making a life for myself. Above all I'm thankful for my female friends, some of whom I met at The Society of Women Writers. We share our troubles which provides solace at times when I'm feeling low. Here you will make life-long friends and find inspiration for your writing.

Pat Curtis

This Frugal Life

My mother-in-law scraped the black from her burnt toast.

The toaster we'd bought her as a Mother's Day present a few years ago was irreparably broken, but she refused to get a replacement.

"I prefer to toast bread over a coal fire the old-fashioned way," she said, smiling.

"But what about during summer when it's hot?" I asked.

"I'll use the grill on the gas stove like I always used to," she said.

My mother-in-law hated to spend money unnecessarily. She was the only person we knew who managed to save money on a government pension!"

We sat in her decrepit kitchen. It had cupboard doors with chipped paint, peeling wallpaper, and we feared for our safety, perched as we were on broken chairs.

"But the toast was actually on fire," I said.

"I enjoy it that way," she said, munching the toast.

"Yesterday you ate the crusts the children left on their plates," I said.

"I abhor waste, and besides I like the crusts."

"What about when you tried to scrape up the smashed egg I dropped on the floor?" I asked.

"I could have made a small omelette," she said, refusing to be goaded.

Several days before, I'd left a few baked beans on my breakfast plate, and she'd insisted: "You must eat every bean."

My husband went through her fridge to prevent anyone getting food poisoning. He'd flung bits of leftover cabbage, potato, and morsels of mouldy cheese into the bin. After discovering dregs of sour milk left in a cup, he threw them away; his mother practically wept, saying, "It would have made a lovely cup of tea."

She was born in 1897 and died in 1990. It had been our task to sort out the contents of the Victorian house in which she'd lived for sixty years. It contained the well-worn, handcrafted mahogany furniture her husband bought when they had moved in.

The drawers were overflowing with brown paper bags, balls of string and rubber bands, and on a long rusty nail were countless receipts, brown with age.

She had lived through the deprivations of two world wars, and the Depression. She was generous to a fault, which annoyed us because, when we gave her presents, she often gave them to needier souls.

She also offered them fantastic home-cooked chicken soup, followed by her apple and blackberry pie made from garden produce.

Unlike her, we never experienced hunger and deprivation. But how cruel we were to make fun of her idiosyncrasies.

Pat Curtis

(Published in Weekend Australian February 2015)

The Angel Next Door

It was a bleak time – Christmas – and Mazy was not looking forward to it. In fact, she dreaded it. It hadn't always been this way though. But now, her daughter no longer spoke to her; her sisters were busy with their families and, when she had attended in the past couple of years, it felt like she was only invited because they felt obligated to invite her. So, this year she had offered to work the Christmas holiday break, which she knew her workmates appreciated.

A knock came on the back door and a blonde head poked around the edge. Mazy really didn't want company. Although she liked the six-year-old neighbour, Kristy could be a handful at times. Bouncing with energy and curiosity, big brown eyes sparkling with mischief, she entered before Mazy could say anything.

"Hi, Mrs Thomas. Mum sent me over to see if you wanted to come over for a coffee. Where is your Christmas tree? Why haven't you got your decorations up? Our tree looks great; I helped Mum and Dad put ours up at the weekend. You have to come and see it."

Mazy felt exhausted as Kristy prattled on. From past experience, she knew the only way to get rid of Kristy was to go next door and have a coffee. She liked her neighbour Anna very much and knew that Anna worried about her, but all Mazy wanted was to be left alone in her sadness and plod through the next few days leading up to the big day.

Sitting over a cup of tea, Mazy explained to Anna that she wouldn't be putting up a tree or decorations this year as she'd be working, and was maybe thinking of going away for a couple of days after Christmas when things at work were back to normal.

Christmas Eve came around, and Mazy was curled up on the couch in her lounge room with a cup of tea and a sandwich when a knock came on the door. As usual, a little blonde head poked around the corner

"Hi, Mrs Thomas. Look what I made for you." Kristy bounced into the room, blonde hair bobbing, eyes twinkling and a huge smile on her face. She held out her hands to Mazy. Mazy gasped not knowing what to say.

"It's a Christmas tree for you. You have to have one, you know; otherwise, Santa won't leave you a present and you have been good."

Mazy smiled and a tear pricked at the edge of her eye. She held her hands out to take the tree, and placed it at the centre of the table. The bright orange tin held a wooden cross, made of two small branches with gold tinsel wrapped across it.

"It's beautiful. Thank you so much." She held her arms out and Kristy fell into them. Never had a hug felt so full of love.

"Come on; Mum's got the kettle on. She said to come and get you for coffee."

They walked hand in hand next door. Kristy took a biscuit and went out the back to play, leaving Mazy and Anna to chat.

"I hope you don't mind the tree. I know it's hideous but Kristy was so upset when you didn't have one. I didn't even know she'd made it until just now, and she is so proud of it."

"It's not hideous; it's the most beautiful tree I've ever had, and it is made with love and I'll cherish it always." And every year it took pride of place on the dining table.

The Christmas spirit is alive and well, thanks to the Angel next door.

Lynne Doyle

The Day Graffy Came to Visit

With aching knees and back, Fee stood and stretched. She'd been weeding the small patch of garden at the front of her house on this warm but overcast day, and perspiration rolled down her neck and down between her ample bosoms.

"Damn." She reached into her shirt and rubbed the affected area of skin, which left a dark smudge of earth. Fee stretched her chubby frame again and looked up at the only surviving bush. She would be able to trim the lower branches; the top ones would be an issue though. Fee loved the bush which sprouted small purple flowers onto the pavement and over her every time she checked the letterbox. "Damn," she said, rubbing her lower back, again forgetting her dirty hands.

"Hi, Gran," came a cheery voice. Fee smiled. Her lovely granddaughter had arrived unexpectedly. Maybe she would have time to help her trim the top of the bush. Much to Fee's surprise, a very tall, four-legged, spotted giraffe was eating the top of the bush.

"What the …? Where did it come from?"

"Don't know – just got off the train and there she was, walking down the street – doesn't seem to have much road sense so I said, 'Come on, Graffy; we'll go to Gran's. You'll be safe and well fed there,' so Graffy followed."

"But … but we can't keep her," spluttered Fee. "You've brought many animals here before but never a giraffe, and you've named her."

"Well, I couldn't leave her to get run over, so here we are."

"I have to admit that Graffy is doing a good job with the bush. I was wondering how I'd get it done. I only hope the flowers don't make her sick. Go and get some water for her, but we'll have to call the ranger to collect her. It's a real mystery how she ended up in Leederville."

By this time a few children and neighbours had gathered to gape and admire Graffy, who was loving the attention; she wasn't alarmed at all.

"I'd better put the kettle on. We can sit at the little table under the eaves while Graffy finishes trimming my bush."

Graffy certainly appeared to be enjoying herself.

Lynne Doyle

It's Your Funeral

During chat, if you say, 'Have you planned your funeral?' within a matter of minutes, you are alone, chatting to the potted palm. If you mention a christening or a wedding, people will surround you. Individuals express interest and give a wealth of advice.

We put great effort into planning life's commemorations: no expense spared. The church has to be right, the flowers, the gowns and the food. Making plans is part of the fun for these events.

So, the word 'interment' will not strike fear, go to an open day at Karrakatta Cemetery. The supervisors are there to address all your queries on burials and cremations.

Funeral professionals today are sympathetic to your wants and needs. It's like planning a wedding. You organise the church, minister, flowers and music. Do you want food and drink for a wake or a simple morning or afternoon tea? Who is doing the eulogies?

A funeral is a one-way, single destination riddle. How you leave this world can be a luxurious event, or simple. Coffins now can be ornate, silk-lined, polished wood or modern painted in your favourite colour. Special Cardboard is in—so everyone can write on it.

Vikings and Egyptians had the right idea, preparations for death put into place on leaving the womb: Vikings in full armour laid out in a vessel, set ablaze by a burning arrow, vanished into the horizon. Egyptian funerals were a grand affair, with more belongings buried with them in the afterlife than they had in the present life.

Formulating your plans for the eventual end makes sense and spares loved ones lots of difficulties when you depart.

When death happens, we have only a few days to arrange a wake, not weeks or months. You can't grumble when sitting up on yon cloud.

"Why that horrible nighty? I should have been in my lovely blue dress!"

"Oh no! She put me in a suit. I wanted me black shorts, singlet, thongs and where's the stubby?"

"Why Chrysanthemums? They knew I have an allergy. I adore red and yellow roses."

Now help is on the Internet with a price, and payment structures, even a 'How to' guide.'

June Earle

Witness

Tick-Tock, Tick-Tock, sounding far then louder. Bruce pushed through the fog; felt agony and compelled himself to open his eyes. Through the table and seat legs, he could see her lying in a crumpled heap on the kitchen floor. She did not flinch, just looked at him, her eyes icy and vacant. Blood oozed from a cut on her head, trickled in rivulets down the face. Bruce edged towards her, paused, lay still. *Two men.* Exhausted, he lay quiet with eyelids shut. He remembered a salty odour … *what else? … what else?*

Tock-Tick, Tock-Tick. The swaying weight on the grandfather clock resounded in the hall. Bruce watched her prepare his evening meal – meat, gravy, and vegetables. It looked so enticing going into the vitamiser – now it looked like mucky custard.

Groaning, he changed into what he hoped would be a more comfortable position; winced – she looked at him.

"You stiffened up again, Bruce? Never mind, tea is ready. It's the weather that gives me arthritis a lot of trouble. We old folk just have to accept it. It tastes better than it looks. Still; there is a lot to be said for having your own teeth."

He loved her, such a gentle soul, as together they plodded through life – he could barely walk with arthritis and she was almost deaf. Bruce would let her know if the doorbell or phone rang. On his good days, he managed a short walk to the shops and helped carry a basket for her. They enjoyed a friendship that bridged their years, each caring for the other's needs.

He listened: *Tick-Tock, Tick-Tock.* Comforted by the gentle beat, he dozed. Woken by a scraping sound, then another, a salty odour stirred his nostrils. She dropped a plate … *clunk, clunk*;

"Where's the money?" The masked man shook her by the shoulders; she rocked back and forth like a rag doll.

"Damn you, old woman, tell me!"

She clawed at the hands around her throat. The pendant fell from the broken chain and rolled towards Bruce. With a furious growl, Bruce struggled to stand, inflamed with rage as he lunged.

"What the …?" The masked man dodged and kicked him, the blow catapulting him across the room.

"NO! NO! Leave him, please." She tried to reach Bruce, but his attacker swung a blow so hard, her balance went and her head connected with the edge of the kitchen dresser. Her precious contents of a dinner service glass jug and ornaments crashed and shattered around her on the floor. The man's accomplice, a tall lanky younger man, burst into the room.

"I've got it. Would you believe the old girl has at least three thousand dollars stuffed in an old gramophone?" His voice trailed off.

"Wow, she looks bad. Is she dead?"

The fellow shrugged. "Don't know, pretty close to it, I'd say."

"How much money did you find?"

The lad snickered. "Well, I didn't count it, but the bag is full."

"What about him?"

"Nothing to worry about. The old boy can walk … full of spunk. He had a go at me before I floored him. I did him a favour. Come on, let's get out of here."

"Hold on a bit. I'll have that locket … should be able to get the chain fixed."

She called his name.

"Bruce, join me." He would join her soon. For now, it was time to pay back all the kindness she had shown him.

He watched as the police came; observed and waited until they came to take her away, murmuring in quiet tones at the tragedy of it all. They walked single file down the hallway past the grandfather clock – *Tick-Tock, Tick-Tock* – through the French doors onto the balcony with its white cane setting and potted greenery. They negotiated the stretcher along the old red brick path, through the pansies, petunias and the prized roses she tended daily. The doors on the ambulance closed then it pulled away from the curb. A diminutive crowd of onlookers bid their silent farewells.

Two men stood under a tree nearby, talking. Bruce knew they were the murderers. He followed them to the docks, watched as they boarded a trawler. The smell of salt hung on the ropes. He watched them mend cray pots; listened to the laughter and their intentions to lie low until it was safe to offload some of the money.

The acne-faced lanky lad kept looking around.

"What's up with you?" the older man asked. Without his mask, his hair and beard were streaked with grey.

"I feel as though we are being watched, and going home last night I could swear someone was behind me."

"Don't let it get to you. No one saw us. There were no witnesses, I made sure of that."

He laughed and his friend joined in.

"I suppose you're right. I'll be glad when we can head out to sea."

The days went by. Now Bruce concentrated on both men. They thought they saw something in the shadows—or did they? The eerie presence left them arguing, uncomfortable and touchy. The younger one could not sleep. He saw himself smashing the gramophone, ecstatic at finding the old lady's hidden cash. His partner in crime kept having flashbacks of the body, her face covered in blood, her cold eyes staring.

Several days later, at the local police station, a constable sought out his sergeant.

"Hey, Sarg, the old lady that was murdered a couple of weeks ago in Maple Street … did she have a big black dog?"

"Yeah, there was a dog … a dead dog was laying alongside her. It was the granddaughter's wish to bury him in the rose garden; she called him Bruce. He had been her grandmother's companion guard dog … a big dog … took two of us to lift him into his grave. Why do you ask?"

"I've got this guy at the front counter, shaking and babbling in a right state. He's confessed to the murder. He's terrified; said the old lady's dog haunts him. The dog knocked his mate down three flights of stairs, resulting in a broken neck. He's given us all the details. It all fits. He even handed in a gold locket. I never imagined I'd see a criminal so desperate to be in prison."

June Earle

Camping

Part 1 - The price of Platapi

We're going camping. It's a first for me. 'You'll see a platypus or two in Broken River, just you wait,' my brother says enthusiastically.

We're a young, and excited foursome. With two two-man tents and minimal gear, we set off in one vehicle from the new mining town of Moranbah in Central Queensland for Eungella National Park for the weekend.

A couple of hours after leaving the tropical heat of the township, our vehicle climbs into the deliciously cool green rolling hills partly obscured by low-hanging clouds. I wind the car window down and breathe in the clean air of the rainforest.

We organise the camp before setting off down a rough track lined with she-oaks and bottlebrush to the river, and single-file, we quietly follow it along, watching the honeyeaters dart, till full access to a wide section opens up. My brother signals, so we sit and wait.

It's real! It's real! I see my first platypus, then my second. I cannot find words to express my wonderment. Whatever would early settlers have made of these strange darting creatures.

Moving away from the river, we continue our walk, this time through low growing ferns and under palms till we find a natural grassed area where we lift our sandwiches and drinks from our backpacks.

'Time to head back before we get caught in the dark,' my

brother advises after we've hiked a few more hours and seen a bush turkey, a snake and birds we couldn't identify.

Back at camp, I collapse onto the waterproof blanket to nurse my poor feet. I'm wearing new hiking boots with my jeans tucked into thick socks. I scratch just above my ankle. There's a lump in my sock. I roll it down.

'Get it off! Get it off!' I scream.

This huge disgusting black thing is stuck to me. I stretch out my leg, hoping someone will chop it off at the knee to relieve me of this slimy attachment.

'Oh, for goodness sake, it's just a leech.' My husband splashes my leg with some rum. Not that I'm watching. I want to be as far away from that leg as I can. My husband and brother are struggling not to laugh at my predicament.

'Look, it's gone now.'

I find the courage to glance at the huge black lump, as big as the upper joint of my little finger, lying motionless on the ground.

'Come on, let's collect firewood.'

The temperature is rapidly dropping. Even though it's summer elsewhere, I've been wearing an old jumper all day. I make a scoop with it and my sister-in-law fills it with medium-sized logs which I dump by the barbeque. The guys cook on this rough brick wood-fired cooker and we stand close for the warmth.

After dinner, as we sit around on the rug yarning, I begin to scratch my tummy. There's no lump, so it's not a leech.

'Show me,' my brother insists.

I pull up my jumper and shirt. There's a tiny black spot.

'It's a tick,' he says.

I'm not as horrified by the tick as I was by the leech, and it backs out of me as he wastes more of my husband's Bundy rum.

A light drizzle begins. 'That does it,' I say. 'I'm off to bed. A leech in the leg and a tick in the tummy has done me in.'

I snuggle into my sleeping bag and read a little by torchlight before falling asleep. My bladder wakes me in the wee-small hours and I struggle quietly from the tiny tent to take a pee. As I push down my jeans I feel a lump on my hip. Oh no, not again!

'A leech, a leech!' I scream.

All three emerge from their tents. It's pitch black, so my husband grabs a torch and inspects where I'm pointing.

'It's a mole. You've always had it,' he grumbles, shaking his head, with the torch highlighting it.

'Sorry.' Sheepishly, I sneak off in the damp weather to relieve myself, while the guys try to re-build the fire. At around 5 am, we have breakfast since everyone's wide awake.

'Want to go home?' my husband asks.

As if he needs an answer.

My brother and his wife acquiesce and we pack as soon as it's light. I climb into the front passenger seat, but before we depart, I feel an itch on my forearm. Pushing up my sleeve, I see this thing walking up my arm by arching its two-centimetre skinny form, then straightening, then arching again. Gross!

I throw my arm out the window, screaming again, 'Get it off, get it off!'

Camping? Me? Never again!

Part 2, Why a toilet roll?

We're going camping again. Just because the first trip ended with a leech in my leg and a tick in my tummy is no reason to give up entirely. Mind you, it took some ten years to recover.

This time we borrow a two-room tent – the second room is to accommodate our five-year-old son and toddler daughter. It's hot and steamy in Central Queensland as we head off to the Isaacs River to meet our friends with their two young boys.

There's nothing spared in this set-up. Loaded in the boot of the 4WD are the picnic table and chairs, barbeque plate, along with all imaginable comforts, including a couple of eskies with ice and cold drinks.

The river is wide, clear and deep, and framed by shady gums. We choose a spot to set up, with a spread of coarse orange sand between us and the creek. I watch my Little One like a hawk since she crawls faster than I walk. Once established, we all dunk ourselves in the water with my Little One clinging to me. It's so warm there's no need to towel off. I rub sunscreen on her and follow it with mozzie repellent. I've seen a few mosquitoes as big as March flies, and their sting, if you're unfortunate enough to be attacked, is just as painful.

The three boys wander off with the three other adults to explore. I'm stuck on the rug with Little One, hoping she'll tire soon and want to sleep. I can't read my book; I must be one hundred percent vigilant.

The gang arrives back with loads of firewood and soon the smell of the sizzling steaks has my saliva glands screaming. I create the illusion of a calm and kind mother, speaking softly and feeding my Little One, but my primal urge is to tie her to a tree and be free of responsibility for a wee while. I should have packed the high chair. We brought everything else. With Little One's bare skin sticking to my sweaty bare skin, speckled with rough grains of sand, I try to eat the steak one-handed. I am hot and cranky, and stay that way for the duration of the afternoon.

Okay, so we listen to some Willie Nelson while we drink a few stubbies, and I cool off in the river occasionally with my little attachment, but it doesn't soothe me.

The sun is fast disappearing. A couple of lanterns give off enough light to prepare for bed. Everyone's been fed again. The temperature has dropped only a few degrees. In spite of that, Little One goes down easily enough, as does five-year-old. I finally get to play adults with the big people. But when it's time for bed, there's that coarse sticky sand stuck to me, especially on my feet. I can't possibly sleep like that. Yuk. Sand between the toes – not likely. I sit in the tent doorway and try to brush it off. I can't wash in the creek. I'd just have to walk through the sand again.

I try to settle wearing just my shorts and tee. The mozzies serenade us. I swat the air around my ears. I get up and use the repellent. It's late. A voice comes from the next room.

'I'm thirsty, Mum.'

I get up and get water for them.

I'm just nodding off.

'I'm hot, Mum.'

'Yes, darling. We'll swim in the morning.'

A hot sticky body crawls on me. Little One.

One hour later. 'I'm thirsty, Mum.'

I nudge my husband. He gets up and swipes a mozzie as he brings water. And so the night becomes a monster.

At first light we're all up. I'd kill for coffee. The fire must be lit first. Thankfully, the men think that's fun.

Little One keeps crawling towards the water through that sticky grainy sand. Every time I pick her up, she and that sand stick to me.

That's it!

'Guys, I'm heading home. That's enough camping for me. You can all stay on and come home in the other Landcruiser.'

The other mum says, 'I'm coming with you.'

'I thought you were having fun?'

'Are you kidding?' I watch her pack enthusiastically, and I do the same.

Once back in the mining town, I drop her off and drive

home, but instead of going inside, I turn the lawn sprinkler on and stand under it with Little One to rid ourselves of that disgusting sand.

One week later, my friend calls in to visit. I'm told later, although I have no memory, that she finds me crawling on the lounge floor with a roll of toilet paper. Apparently, I'm delirious.

The doctor orders blood tests.

'Been anywhere where you might have been bitten by mosquitoes?' he asks once I'm coherent.

Results show I have contracted Ross River virus. Nasty. It lingers. A third camping trip is definitely not on my agenda.

Part 3 - The Antidote

Ten years have passed since the last camping trip. With determination to succeed at this camping business, from Perth I organise a family safari in Kakadu for ten days. I choose a tour guide whose speciality is Aboriginal culture.

He puts forth an exciting itinerary showing he is able to access regions other tours cannot, adding, 'Any specific requests?'

My clear responses are: a hot shower every night where I don't get my feet dirty, sheets on the camp bed, protection from mozzies, and chamomile tea.

Day one, early evening: As our guide's offsider prepares hors d'oeuvres, we sit at the camp table covered in a white sheet adorned with two empty beer cans holding lit candles. They understand my needs and we dine well.

Our guide tells our fifteen-year-old son that he's about to turn him from a lily-livered city slicker into a bush-bashing bastard.

'There's no hope for you, Mother,' he adds, passing him the pannikin to give to me. 'That's her hippie tea.'

After dinner, he hoists the black plastic bag full of hot water up into a tree. The bag spent the day on the roof of the Landcruiser. He drapes a screen of hessian around and places two black rubber mats on the ground. One's for showering on, the other for standing on to towel dry and put footwear on. Now I'm camping.

And I'm ready for anything the next day, including paddling upstream to Jim Jim Falls. We swim in the waterhole with the freshwater crocodiles, and lunch on chicken and champagne towed upstream in a waterproof drum.

The tour guide needs to call into Jabiluka to acquire a special pass for Arnhem Land. While we wait, we join an audience sitting cross-legged on the grass in front of an older Aboriginal man leaning on a low timber fence. He's not easy to understand, but we listen attentively. I later learn his name is Bill Neidjie and he's a deeply respected elder of the Gagudju people. We misunderstood the pronunciation and called the place Kakadu.

Noticing our interest, our guide begins to read to us from Bill's book, *Story about Feeling*. Well, not really his book, since Bill neither reads nor writes, but he speaks wild wisdom, which someone, with Bill's permission, has captured and recorded. Bill doesn't understand why white fellas need to cover the sky with a tent. He doesn't understand why white fellas need to drive over small trees instead of going around them like black fellas do. 'Everything's coming up Toyota', he says.

With our pass, we travel to Nourlangie Rock in Arnhem Land, where we walk single file up the aisle on soft brown soil, with guinea grass two metres high on either side, towards the rock. I experience the same tingling sensation as I did walking down the aisle in Westminster Abbey. We arrive at our destination, and, as instructed, lie on our backs on the flat reddish rock to stare at the paintings on the overhanging shelf high above. 'They're Mimi spirits up there,' the guide tells us as we gaze at the stick figures, 'dating back twenty thousand plus years.' No one can work out how they got up there as there are no supports to access the overhang.

Day after day we left in a state of wonder as we are transformed by our experiences.

I even begin to help assemble the tents at night and dabble with cooking. Finally, I have conquered this camping quest!

Shirley Elridge

Four Seasons

Early summer morning as I walk up the hill
light breezes caress my face
gently ruffling my hair.
Birds twitter.
Hissing sprinklers
dancing in the wind
lighten my step.
On the lush lawns
sparkling diamonds glitter
where sprinklers have played.

Early autumn mornings as I walk up the hill
grey shrouds envelope me.
Mist in the air
blurs all sharpness.
The ocean is veiled
by a mass of faded, grey cotton.
Shafts of sunlight jolt me
out of my reverie
bringing promise
of a glorious day after all.

Early winter mornings as I walk up the hill
cold winds catch my breath
numb my fingers, tingle my ears.
Snuggling into my cosy coat
I trudge up the hill
turning to taste the soft sky hues
of red, pink and blue
against the still ocean.
Another crystal morning.
A breath of freshness.

Early spring mornings as I walk up the street
the sun's blanket
shields me from cold ocean winds.
Buds peep eagerly, flowers sway gracefully
showing off colourful robes.
Snails glide across footpaths
leaving glitter in their wakes.
Spring is in the air
lovingly spreading
Her wonderful glow.

Malini Green

The poem Four Seasons was highly commended in the Edith Fisher Memorial Award competition, judged by the Sun City Writers Group. It was published in the Wanneroo Times (May 6-12 2003 Edition)

A Boy's Dream

24 December 1957 8pm

'Mummy, I don't want to sleep.'

Maria dries her hands and turns away from the kitchen sink. 'No? Why not?' She picks up her son and carries him upstairs, back to his bedroom.

'Because tomorrow is Christmas!' he replies. His smile stretches from ear to ear, and Maria can't help but smile back. 'I can't wait to see Santa and open my presents.'

'But the sooner you fall asleep, the quicker tomorrow will come.' She sits him on the side of his bed and strokes his soft hair from his eyes. 'What are you hoping Santa will bring you?'

'More toy soldiers, a submarine and a toy gun!' He points his fingers out in the shape of a pistol and shoots his mum. She puts her hand on her heart and leans back, pretending to be injured. 'I want to be just like Daddy and fight for my country one day.'

'If you work hard, you can.' Maria smiles and bends down to tuck him in. 'Now sleep.' She hopes his dream will come true. It will be a proud day indeed. She kisses him before standing and closes his curtains. An icy shiver runs down her back and she tightens her dressing gown. 'Good night, son. Sweet dreams.' She turns off the light but leaves his door open a little.

14 March 1975 10am

'You will not sleep,' the sergeant informs his troop. It is one of the ten commandments being drilled into the new recruits. He realises he must obey the orders to do well and progress up the ranks. The KGB is not for weak men. Only those with physical and mental strength survive in the organisation. Does he have what it takes to make it all the way and realise his childhood dream to fight for his country?

28 July 1983 11.45pm

'I love you, Lyudmila.' He takes her by the hand and leads her into their bedroom. She sits on the edge of the bed and he gives her a smouldering kiss on her lips. He kisses her along her neck and across her shoulders. His hands find their way under her satin slip dress. She helps him remove it while fumbling with the zip of his pants. Clothes scatter on the carpet while the newlyweds discover each other's bodies for the first time. Lyudmila sleeps soon after; her rhythmic breathing is music to his ears. He rests his hand on her breast and stares at the wall. Not wanting to sleep, he savours the beauty in this moment. He promises to make her proud and will do everything he can to keep her safe.

28 April 1985 1am

'Ambulance please,' he screams into the phone. 'My wife's in labour!' He puts the receiver down and the paramedics arrive a short time later.

'Her waters broke about an hour ago, and contractions are three minutes apart,' he informs them.

'Your first child?' they enquire.

'Yeeesss,' Lyudmila screams, as another contraction starts.

'Can't you give her something for the pain?' he asks while she squeezes his hand.

'We need to get her to the hospital first,' they explain.

They all climb into the back of the ambulance. With lights flashing and sirens blaring, they arrive at the hospital a short time later. As the sun rises, Lyudmila gives birth to a healthy daughter.

They can barely keep their eyes open. But when they meet her for the first time, their smiles show relief and happiness.

'Let's call her Mariya,' he suggests.

Lyudmila nods in agreement. A tear escapes her eye. They vow to watch over her at all times and do everything they can to ensure a safe future for their new family.

26 March 2000 9.30pm

Cheering, clapping and whistles fill the room as the President Elect takes to the stage. He gestures for the crowd to hush, and addresses his supporters and the waiting global media.

'Ladies and gentlemen, today we had a victory. The people have voted. I will be your supreme leader: the divine leader of the eastern world. I will work hard from the Kremlin, and will fight for what Russians deserve.'

The crowd applauds. Cameras click, flashing lights filling the room like a disco ball.

He continues. 'I want to thank my parents, my wife and daughters. I hope I have made you all proud. My people are my family. I promise to serve my country and keep every Russian man, woman and child safe from harm.'

Everyone claps and cheers. 'Tonight we will celebrate our win. But from Monday, we will be working hard for this country!'

They party hard, drinking White Russians into the early hours of the next morning.

16 April 2009 6pm

Waving flags in the air, Russians line the streets as troops returning from Chechnya parade down the main street. Their leader, a hero for leading them to victory, stands with his head poking out of an army tank. He waves to the crowd. There are women with their children who are relieved to have their husbands home again, and older people who are glad to have their sons back on home soil. Their leader hasn't slept much in the last month for the battlefield was brutal. Smiling to the crowd, he savours the atmosphere. He is looking forward to seeing his family again and sleeping in his own bed. But first, there is so much to do that sleep is far from his mind.

23 February 2022 8pm

'Sir, with all due respect, will you not be retiring tonight?' the secretary asks the President.

He looks up over his computer screen. 'We have important work to do tonight. Our forces are lined up on the border of Ukraine. Tomorrow we begin our march across, and take what belongs to us.'

'But, are you sure it's the right thing to do? Couldn't you try negotiating or ...'

'It is the only thing left to do.' He stands up and looks the secretary in the eye. 'That land is ours. We must fight for it.' He slams his fist on his desk as he sits again, clanging coffee cups and other items.

'As you wish, President Putin,' the secretary replies. 'I'm here if you need anything.'

Melanie Hawkes

Autumn Leaves

She places her bag of meagre belongings on the seat. *This will do for tonight,* she thinks. The park is now empty. Families have gone home early to their warm houses. The children are no longer frolicking in the giant piles of leaves.

The woman reaches into her bag, searching for snacks. Her fingers find a muesli bar; the wrapper is still sealed, so she figures it is safe to eat. That is despite finding it on the school oval after lunch. Those kids are lucky to have several meals a day and a warm bed. How lucky she is for finding food at all.

She savours every bite and swallows slowly. After throwing away the empty wrapper, she tries to ignore the loud grumbling coming from her belly. It has taken her a while to get used to the constant hunger pains. Nobody warned her about that when she lost her house. The sky turns the colour of roasted pumpkin, matching the colour of the fallen leaves. It will be dark soon, so she finds a thick pile of leaves and gets down on the ground. She makes a pillow out of more leaves and pulls her sheet of cardboard over her like a doona. If she wakes up in the morning, she will search in bins for containers to get some money for a decent meal. And hopefully have enough coins left over to wash her clothes. Nobody wants to hire her the way she looks. But she desperately wants a job so she can get a house and have her kids back again soon.

And if she doesn't wake up, may a kind person find her, and give her a fitting farewell. She'd prefer she wasn't left to rot like the pile of leaves that has become her comforting bed this evening.

Melanie Hawkes

Daddy's Girl

You were there when I was born, and when I learnt to walk. My first word was 'Dad'. You took me to school on my first day; saw me graduate from university.

Then you found me my first job; and walked me down the aisle. One day you said you were being deployed. We cried at the airport; wrote letters regularly. I sent photos of Jack when he was born.

Mum called me when she heard you'd stepped on a land mine and were not coming home. Now I wear the poppy with pride; to honour your sacrifice for our freedom.

Melanie Hawkes

Froot Loops

"You don't want your froot loops this morning?"

My son drops his spoon in his bowl and shakes his head.

"Why not?" I ask. "I thought they were your favourite."

"Lisa at school said Scott Morrison is a froot loop," he replies. 'I'm not eating the old prime minister."

I pick up his bowl and try a spoonful. "You're right," I say, while tipping the rest in the bin. "It does leave a bad taste in your mouth."

Melanie Hawkes

Machines Strike Back

Waiting, waiting. That is all Walter does most days. Is that all he is good for now?

Business has all but dried up lately, ever since Harvey Norman had a sale last month. Half price washing machines! How dare they? Nobody needs to use our coin laundry any more. It's not fair. Who has coins these days anyway? People with their fancy Fitbits and PayPass cards, what's society coming to? People won't remember what it's like to sit and talk to each other, and wait for their washing to finish.

"Is that Mrs Jones with her boy Timmy who just walked past?" asks Daisy.

"Why, you might be right!" Walter replies. "Nothing wrong with your eyesight!"

"How tall he's grown! How old would he be now, Walter?"

"Let's see, we'd only been here a year or two when his older sister was born, and that was before Irina arrived here."

"Did someone say my name?" Irina asks. Pressed for time, she'd prefer not to be drawn into gossip and chit-chat with the others. Flat out, she likes to think she is.

"Yes, Irina, how long have you been here?" Daisy asks.

"Probably about six years now. I worry about being upgraded for a newer model."

"Don't we all?" Walter remarked and everyone whirred in agreement. "That makes Timmy about five then. Already at school. How quickly they grow. Feels like yesterday that we were washing his dirty bibs and clothes."

"I feel sorry for Mrs Jones," Daisy pipes up.

"What for?" Walter asks.

"I'm sure her good-for-nothing husband is having an affair with Emily, the new young girl in the bank."

"How dare he! I'll kick him – oh, is that why he's been in here more often lately?"

"Probably. He's our biggest paying customer at the moment. Come to think of it, could've been our only customer this week. Trying to have her scent taken out of his shirts before he goes home." Daisy pauses, before continuing. "I'm curious to know what he sees in Emily. Mrs Jones deserves better."

"How about we sort him out next time? I'll eat one of his socks. Daisy, you conk out just before his shirts are dry. Irina, you run out of steam so his collar won't press as nicely and Patrick, you listening?" Walter asks.

"Huh? Are you talking to me?" Patrick replies. "People usually curse me as I'm always taking their money. I switch off once they've paid."

"Yes, Patrick, well, listen up. When Mr Jones comes in smelling like Emily, we need you to not only take his money, but not give him any change either, ok?" Walter tells him.

"Ok, Walter, I am sure I can manage that," Patrick replies. "But will your plan work? It could make them go somewhere else."

"Better not. That place across town already closed down, I think. I'm sure he'll come clean with her soon."

Melanie Hawkes

My Fantasy Life

'What do you think you would be doing if you weren't in a wheelchair?' I get asked this quite often. It's fun to fantasise about the life I might have had if I didn't have my disability.

Would I be married? Possibly. My husband would be tall, fit and handsome. Maybe Spanish. Our wedding would have been outdoors in a beautiful garden, perhaps in the grounds of a winery. My dress would've been full length, with a lace-covered train following me as my dad walked me down the aisle. I would've had three bridesmaids wearing purple dresses, to match the purple irises in my bouquet.

Would I be a mum? I think I would have had two children: a girl and a boy. They'd grow up speaking Spanish as well as English. My parents would love more grandchildren.

What work would I be doing? It would have to be a part-time job, during school hours. It might be in a bakery, or a small cafe. I love food and socialising. Definitely not office work. I don't think I'd have been the type to sit down all day.

Would I be living in the country or the city? Possibly on a farm, with chickens for eggs, some sheep, a pig, and a dog or three. And a horse of course, for the kids to ride. Also, fruit trees and vegetable gardens, and compost bins.

What car would I drive? Not a van, maybe a jeep. They're good for getting around the paddocks. But I'd need a better car for trips to the city. Maybe a purple V-Dub Beetle. I've always loved those.

What would I do in my spare time? Trampolining and rock-climbing would be fun, as would bush walking. But between taking my daughter to dance and my son to football training, there probably wouldn't be much time to do those things. Perhaps I would knit or crochet in the evenings after my kids were in bed.

Would I have travelled the world? Gone backpacking through Europe maybe, picking up bits and pieces of the different languages along the way, and my husband. I had a trip to England once, but the cobblestones were so bumpy in my wheelchair.

It's fun to fantasise, but the truth is my wheelchair has given me many opportunities. Without my disability, I wouldn't have been a little Telethon star and met Stevie Wonder when I was seven years old.

I wouldn't have won a scholarship to study Japanese at university. I might not have gone on exchange to Japan for a year when I was nineteen. Even if I had, I wouldn't have become famous. Every Japanese newspaper and TV station covered my year there, challenging the beliefs about what people with disabilities are capable of.

I might not have become an interpreter and worked in hospitals, court rooms or schools. Facilitating the communication between both parties was always met with gratitude. It was great being paid to talk.

I may not have started bonsai, a hobby I really enjoy. Some of my trees have been in local exhibitions and I am always keen to learn more at workshops and conventions. Bonsai has definitely fuelled my creativity and my appreciation of nature.

I wouldn't have been part of a disability awareness campaign when I was twenty-five. A poster of me was on bus stops all over the place, as well as a commercial on TV. For several years after, I couldn't wear the same clothes, lest I be recognised.

I wouldn't have been invited onto committees and boards. I

really enjoyed the Department of Transport's Access Advisory Committee, looking at access on stations, train carriages and low-floor buses. As these improvements were made, it was great seeing people out and about, using them with ease.

I wouldn't have got my job at the Department of Fire and Emergency Services nineteen years ago. I enjoy my two days a week there. How does everyone work five days a week with only two off? It's much better the other way around. I wouldn't have my second job either, providing advice on digital access issues.

I wouldn't have had three amazing assistance dogs. My current dog Upton, a Labrador cross Golden Retriever, has very good skills. He can take my shoes and socks off, pick up things that I drop, open and close doors, fill my washing machine and get my lunch out of the fridge. We even pick up litter while we're out walking. Although he had to retire early due to anxiety, I couldn't live on my own without his assistance.

Sure, there have been times when I wish I could walk, take myself to the toilet or scratch an itch on my foot. I can fantasise about not being in a wheelchair, but without my disability, I would not be who I am today.

Melanie Hawkes

The Perfect Cookie Recipe

Hi there! It's Rebecca, the YouTuber, back here and today I have a killer recipe for you: peanut butter and chocolate chip cookies. These will make everyone come begging for more. International Cookie Day might be over for another year, but you can try these out any time. You need:

1 cup of peanut butter – you want the one with xylitol for extra sweetness

half a cup of brown sugar

half a cup of wholemeal flour

1 egg

half a teaspoon of baking soda

1 cup of dark chocolate chips, the darker the better

A handful of raisins or sultanas

Alright, I'm ready to begin. Follow along at home.

First, preheat a fan-forced oven to 180°C and line a baking tray. You want the oven nice and hot, and the fan helps to drown out the noise of the dogs next door, right? You know the ones that bark all day and distract you while working from home, and all night while trying to sleep. Yep, they're driving me mad.

Next, mix the sugar, peanut butter, egg and baking soda together in a stand mixer on medium speed until combined. 'Cos the mixer and the oven fan combined is even louder than the barking over the fence. But if you don't have one, use a wooden spoon and stir like crazy. Just like my Aunt Joanne went after her boyfriend left her – crazy. Not heard from her since. She might be in a hospital for the insane. I'll end up there if the dogs don't shut up soon. But I digress. Got it all combined? Good. Fold in the chocolate chips. Remember they should be dark choc, not milk, and a good handful of raisins. Just like this, and maybe a few extra choccy chips, 'cos they're so deadly. I might eat a couple now - yum!

Step three:

You can either make small balls or roll and cut out shapes. The mixture should be soft and doughy. I have a heart-shaped cookie cutter that makes the cutest cookies. You can make those for your boyfriend, or your girlfriend. Just not your best friend, if they're wagging a tail. You can make round ones with your hands if you prefer. Work it with your fingers. Pretend it's your stress ball, as those dogs just won't shut up and you're getting more and more annoyed. Or the time your boss gave you a report to edit by the next day and you spent all night working on it, and missed your boyfriend's mum's birthday dinner, and now she won't talk to you. I'm sure you get what I mean. Stress isn't fun, but baking cookies sure is! Right, I'm done, these go on the baking tray you prepared earlier. Leave a gap in between each one. You want cookies, not a slice.

Next step, four I think we're up to:

Bake in the oven for about 12 minutes. Long enough to make a coffee and relax for a bit. Still no peace and quiet with the dogs next door barking, but I'll turn on some music. I love the baking smell in the house. It's like a delicate perfume, just delicious. Hope you're going to enjoy these at home too. See you back here in a bit. Don't go away!

Hi, I'm back. They should have a golden glow when they're done, so remove the cookies from the oven. Allow them to rest for five minutes before transferring them to a rack to cool completely. Try keeping your family's razor-sharp eyes off these while you wait. I know it's hard, like trying to make a phone call while the dogs are barking, but it'll be worth it. I promise.

Rebecca would never lie to you.

And that's it. Bon Appétit!

They'll keep in a cookie jar for a few weeks, but they won't last long – they're too delicious. Avoid sharing them with your dog, even though she'll drool at the smell of the cookies. However, and here's the best part: you can easily throw a cookie over the fence every time you hear the neighbour's dogs bark. 'Cos you know you're sick of hearing them all day and all night. Be generous, you can always make more for yourself. The owners are never home; they won't know. And when the dogs finally go silent and still, you'll have the peace and quiet you deserve. If the owners come around and ask what happened, just tell them you were only sharing your homemade cookies – and give them some to take home!

Melanie Hawkes

Editor's Note: Do not feed dogs chocolate or raisins as it can be fatal. Get it?

To My Sweetheart

It was love at first sight. Although it was many years ago, my love for you has not waned. In fact, it's now stronger and deeper than ever. I am truly and madly in love with you, and I still have trouble keeping my hands off you.

When I brought you home, I couldn't wait to undress you. As I stripped you, the aroma hit me and made me giddy with excitement. Short, dark and handsome, your heavenly contours greeted my eyes. My heart swelled with each tender caress of you. I licked the length of your body; your touch was cool and smooth on my lips. Immense pleasure filled me, while my tastebuds danced with anticipation. Never had I feasted on anything as exquisite. Your creamy exterior melted on impact.

I bit you. A thousand pieces scattered around my mouth and I savoured the delicious taste of every morsel. I couldn't resist taking another bite, but nothing prepared me for what happened next. The taste sensation was next level.

Clenched between my lips, I plunged you into my cup and sucked hard. To my surprise and utter delight, chocolate-flavoured milk flooded my mouth. It was the most amazing sip of milk I had ever experienced; nothing else has come close to impressing me since. I swallowed the liquid, then gobbled you up whole. Your crunchy middle had become a soft and gooey delight.

"Yes, yes, yes!" I yelled. Hopefully my neighbour hadn't heard my screams of pleasure.

I may have flirted with different flavours, but you will always be my favourite, and are the only one I buy now. You have caused me grief with my weight, but you bring me joy. There is no better treat in this world than a Double Coat Tim Tam Slam. Happy Valentine's Day, my sweetheart.

121

Melanie Hawkes

Ukraine

Bullets fire, bombs fall, missiles strike
Horrific images glow on my TV
The Russian army invades Ukraine
Into neighbouring countries they flee

Mothers, fathers, sons and daughters
Their lives will never be the same
World leaders imposed sanctions on Russia
Yet are powerless to stop Putin's game

Ukrainian men join the army
As their wives and children shelter
Buildings fall, bridges are bombed, many die
Essentials are scarce, like food, heat and water

Worldwide governments send supplies
To fight the Russians out of Ukraine
I watch the news and hope and pray
That peace can be restored again

Melanie Hawkes

Buzzing

The Blue-Banded Bee hovers
buzz-pollinating capsulated flowers
returning pollen to her nest
before the summer day rises,
hurrying as the heat encroaches,
forcing her to hide beneath the earth.

The little Aussie bee watches
As rosellas suck nectar from pillars
of ancient grass trees.
In towering safety, the birds reside
In early morn marking seasons tide,
before temperatures start to rise.

November rains arrive by chance
Providing refreshing sustenance.
Nuytsia floribunda erupts orangy bright
shining like a beacon in the sunlight
announcing scorching days
And the beginning of Christmas.

Ann Hunter

Wheatbelt Antics

Dazzling canola dances in the wind
revealing grassy she-oak patches
where a white spider orchid grows,
a refugee from the field of yellow
amongst the granite outcrop row.

Clutching sandy wheatbelt soils
the spindly hairy orchid toils,
wooing a male thynnine wasp
with its red labellum clasp,
which flies off with precious cargo.

The happy wasp waxes lyric,
when he is attracted by a spider mimic.
Later a tiny green shoot emerges,
avoiding the oblivious sheep nearby
that grazes on Spring grasses.

Ann Hunter

hoops

You
train me
to jump through hoops
wear flowers in my aura
flaunt feathers and finery
to lift the eyes from tattered skirts
you dress me in

I
spin within your hoops
camouflage my thoughts with joyful smiles
wear purple warmers on my wrists
to hide the scars
caused by your eternal domination

You
spruik to crowds
who watch my daily act
watch me spinning in your rule
gyrating to your constant requirements
as I lose my identity
in an ocean of regret
and fix the smile rigid
to hide the thoughts within

I
founder
torn between first love and marital duty
wrestle with a pride too long suppressed
and try to stay afloat
knowing that all you see
is the size of the ring that binds me
never knowing that …

You
are the hole in my boat
and
I
drown
'neath the weight of your expectations

Helen Iles

Neither Lie, Douglas

Two tousled-headed boys were sitting on the curb of their leafy suburban street, one keenly watching the traffic that whizzed by on the busy intersection further up, the other studying a puddle that had been left from the recent rains, taking particular note as a silent plummeting droplet from the overhanging tree above plopped and disturbed its surface. He leaned further forward over his knees, catching the other boy's attention.

"What are ya doin', Douglas?" the second boy enquired with a frown.

"Readin' puddles," came the youngster's droll reply.

"How do ya read puddles?" the enquirer smirked again. "Ya can't even read. Ya too young."

"I can read puddles!" Douglas quipped back offendedly, scratching at the freckle line across his nose.

"How?!" came the scoffing remark. "Show me how!"

"It's easy," the little boy said. "You just have to look. Just look into the water and you can see all sorts of things."

The older boy leaned forward sceptically. "Like what?"

Douglas waited for the ripples to clear, waited for the smooth reflection to cast its vision before his eyes then he started reading – the only reading his young age was capable of. "I can see a tree," he said. "It's a street tree, all green an' yellow an' wet. And it's going to be a big tree." A drip-stirred ripple clouded the pool for a second then all was still again.

"I can see a blue sky," the little boy advised next, "an' it's clear so there won't be any more rain today." They were wise words from an only just five-year-old, and the other boy looked up in verification, sensed there was more to this puddle reading than met the eye, and leaned forward closer.

"I can see you," Douglas said, turning his head to look straight at the ten-year-old, a hint of affection showing.

"Yeah? And what can ya tell about me?"

"The puddle says Andrew will be my friend." He looked up hopefully, yet caught the other boy's face hardening a little.

"Did it now?!" came the teasing retort, but he had caught the despairing plea from the lonely little boy who had just moved in next door.

"Uh huh. The puddle says so ... an' puddles don't lie." He shook his head earnestly.

"How do ya know that?!"

Douglas's face tightened in defence. "My Daddy says so. Puddles don't lie!" His voice was adamant.

"Okay ... okay," the older boy pacified him without commitment. "So what else do you see?" he dodged the subject.

"Sometimes I see Mummy's face in the puddle."

Andrew frowned again. All the things the little boy had seen had actually been there, and he flashed a quick and worried glance behind them to Douglas's house.

"But you can't. I heard she's ..."

"I can!" Douglas protested. "I can see her! Daddy said I can! An' I see her in the puddles ... any time I want!"

Andrew detected immediately the great sense of loss the little boy was feeling. He'd lost his dog in the year just gone and although it wasn't quite the same, he understood that sense of being so alone.

"... an' if it's not raining, I can see her in the clouds," Douglas prattled hurriedly, desperate to convince the other boy.

"Yeah. I know ... She's an Angel, isn't she?" Andrew said, remembering how his parents had handled his grief.

"Uh huh. Daddy said so."

Andrew rose to his feet, stepped back from the curb as the school bus rounded the corner to his street. He pulled Douglas up and moved him back a safe distance.

"Well, puddles and Daddy's don't lie, Dougie. They don't lie," Andrew smiled as the bus braked beside him. "I'll see you after school, matey."

Douglas smiled back, first at Andrew, then as the bus pulled away and the puddle cleared, at his mother's fading reflection.

Helen Iles

Power of the Sea

Surging
Swirling
bubbling wash of cyanic green boast
Churning
Ebbing
Sweeping in to crash upon the rocky coast
Funnelling
Gushing
an angry insurgent
Booming
through the chasm in resounding voice
Splattering
its very existence
in a spume of shattered atoms.
No choice.

Then courses back to renew its wrath
alive, and beating,
breathing ocean,
Sending
heartbeats pounding with emotion.

You are a trap
Yet what draws our minds?

Mesmerised,
I fall into your spell
and fall into the Albany Gap;
into the crushing tide.

Just another countless suicide.

Helen Iles

Singing Blackwood

She stands centre stage, swaying to the music, the bright park lights behind her haloing her head like an angel's as she strums her old guitar. She sings, sweet words pouring out on her misty breath into the night, beautiful songs that seep out into the crowd. She gazes down at the mesmerised faces staring up at her, at the smiles that appear through crisp chill as people clap every melody – that they are still here on this damp night tells her she has made it, even if only on this small park platform in Central Park. But it's not accolades she seeks – she prays for something else in the crowd, a familiar face she's been longing to find most of her life.

As one song ends, she begins another, the crowd soon fading from her thoughts as she drifts back along the road that brought her to this place, a road of twisting turns through long rolling hills, a road that skirts wide, winding streams, where sunlight mottles her face and night's chandelier and the rock and roll of the bus coax her to sleep. As stars now twinkle in the dark sky over the city, she could almost smell the flowers growing along that roadside, flowers that stretched across her garden and massed below the white-railed porch out the front of her house. She saw the porch again, where she'd sat cross-legged, young hands shuffling through handwritten lyrics as she looked for the next song to play.

"Sing Blackwood Hill," Grandpa would say.

Always Blackwood Hill. He was her only audience back then, and he would sit and tell her stories of when he used to play the old flat-top guitar he had given her, every story different from the last, every time changing subtly. Her mamma had said not to believe him, for he'd given his old guitar to her father a long time ago, and she didn't know where it was now. But this old guitar she cherished, even if it wasn't Grandpa's own. She would play it for hours on the verandah, occupying him as she strived for the purest of notes, and he'd heartily applaud every single song.

"Bravo, bravo!" he'd say, "Play another one! Play Blackwood Hill, Cherry."

"Don't encourage her, Dad," her mother would scold. "I don't want her head filled with that rubbish you told her father. She needs to be off doing other things."

But all she had ever wanted to do was play this guitar and sing, and all her mother did was enrol her in netball and painting classes, and invite her friends over to play jacks and hopscotch. She had soon used them more wisely than that.

From the platform of her tree house, she would perform for them, singing and strumming to her heart's content. Grandpa would sit in the shade of the spreading branches beneath her stage, and tap his foot to the beat, while her mother scowled from the verandah. When she'd finished singing, Grandpa would toss a handful of candy and her friends would clap and whistle, the louder the applause, the bigger the handful of sweets. She would kiss him on the forehead after her daily performance. "I love you, Grandpa," she'd say, and he'd reply: "They'll be here tomorrow same time. You need the practice."

She gazes down now, her big blue eyes searching the crowd, and realises her closeness to the edge of her stage, something she'd learnt to check after she'd fallen from the deck of the tree house once and broken her arm. She'd been unable to play for months – in that time, she could only sing.

"Will you take that infernal noise elsewhere," her mother would yell. "Down by the river preferably!"

She'd met Willy James that year down by the river. He was two years older than her and became her very best friend. He'd be waiting for her wherever she went – by her locker in the hall of Blackmore High – by the fountain outside the music room – outside the music store where she'd buy tattered sheet music because that's all she could afford. Not that she could read music – it was the lyrics she wanted – the tune she'd play by ear, even if she did fumble at times with the chords. Willy didn't mind the many times she fumbled, and sometimes she made so many stuff-ups they would laugh with gusto till they fell from their favourite rock and tumble onto the ground.

In the wintertime, Willy took sick. She was asked to play at his funeral. She played at Grandpa's funeral too. He'd bought her a new guitar in the months before he'd passed, and the house had become fuller of arguments.

In her final year at school, her mother threw a hissy-fit that broke all chance of treating each other civilly. "Forget it, Cherry. You're not even good at it, let alone brilliant! Your grandfather should never have encouraged you. You've wasted your whole damn life doing this, just like your father has!"

She'd stayed in her room after that, learning her songs in solitude, singing them softly, planning, sneaking down to the river where she and Willy had sat, singing Reba McIntyre songs loudly to the ducks and geese that silently slid by. Sometimes they would linger before pushing off downstream, which was better than no audience at all. How she missed Grandpa now. How she missed Willy. And Lord, how she wanted to follow those ducks downstream.

That Spring, she took a job at Walt's corner store, selling the heart-shaped candy, bubblegum and humbugs Grandpa used to toss to her friends. She liked the candy store – it reminded her of Grandpa – and it provided her with money which she spirited away in a jar in her closet, saving for her rainy day. It came in the June of her seventeenth year.

The skies fairly opened up and poured freedom over her as she boarded a Greyhound bus going anywhere. There she sat, gazing out the misty back window, watching intently in case her mother came driving after her. She revelled in the joy as the sun came out, daubing her face with light as she watched the rolling green hills roll less and less until they flattened in the sunset. She wondered in that moment of sadness if this was how her father had felt when he'd packed up and left, Grandpa's old guitar maybe propped up on his knee, as hers was. Or did the excitement of chasing his dream override all thoughts of never going home again? She'd wiped a tear and settled in for the long ride to her future, in whatever city that would be. One day, she'd vowed, when she'd made it big, she'd return, even if just to show her mother how wrong she'd been.

Right now though, she turns her collar to the wind and looks up behind her. The bright lights blind her momentarily, but she sees beyond them to the thick clouds gathering overhead and sees and feels the minute beads of moisture drifting on the air. She worries that the crowd will drift as well, ruining her moment, and wonders if her father ever suffered nights like this, the open air dampening his hair, chilling his throat, making his voice raw and raspy. On nights like this, when he didn't know where he would sleep that night, did he ever want to pack up his kit and go home?

She'd gone home once, years after she'd left. She'd walked along her long and leafy street, loitered beneath the arms of the old spreading elm to watch a young girl sitting cross-legged on her verandah. The girl had shuffled scattered pages, then played soft, mournful notes on a violin that made her sigh deeply. Her mother had moved, it seemed, given up on her ever coming home; given up on her father; gone where she didn't have to hear the music that constantly taunted her.

She'd walked along the river then, sat on *their* rock, visited Willy and Grandpa, and vowed to show that he was right and her mother was wrong, that they were right to chase their dreams. Grandpa had always been sad that he hadn't.

Everywhere she worked on the road, she listened for her father's name, wondering if he'd changed it. Maybe he was up on the big stage somewhere, and she didn't even know. How would she know him if he was? Sometimes she looked for her mother in the crowd, hoping she would one day understand, hoping she would one day try to mend the fences she had built between them over the years. She hoped her mother would realise that her fears of her leaving like her father had actually driven her away.

She sniffs now as a chill wind strikes her back, absently brushes raindrops from the polished wood of Grandpa's gift guitar. It is almost time to pack it in its case to protect it from the cold night air. But while there is a crowd, there is music. She shuffles through her mind for more words and more chords, for something to hold them longer. Her fingers ache from the cold, but still she strums the cold metal strings, which warms her fingertips.

"Hey, Blondie! … do you know Blackwood Hill?" a voice comes from beyond the shifting crowd.

She looks up over the damp, relocating bodies and peers through the gloom. "I know Blackwood Hill," she nods, and commands the strings to harmonise in the opening chords. The man moves closer, a man handsome for his age, a man with the most crystal-clear blue eyes she'd ever seen. "My grandfather taught it to me," she says.

He grins. "My father taught it to me. Here, look," he said, looking up, "it's starting to rain. Put that guitar away and come down off that wall. There's not enough people here in this park worth destroying a good instrument for."

She welcomes his logic, beds the guitar down in its velvet case and closes the lid. There will be other nights to sing.

"Come, do you want to get a coffee - one poor musician's offer to another?" The man swings his battered guitar bag off his shoulder. "We need to put a bit of heat back in our bones."

She nods, connecting immediately to the kind face and warm smile, to the friendly voice and casual manner. She wonders if he feels the same. By his look, he does.

In a cafe across the street, they talk, compare street savvy, stay out of the rain. How to find the right location in the park is important. Changing it on days to chase the crowd is just as critical. She has learnt that. How to live on the meagre coins and notes tossed into their cases is difficult; how to hold onto the dream of making it big even harder. The rain stops, and they shoulder their baggage, shake coffee-warmed hands and walk in opposite directions. The lights cast long shapes on the pavement, moving the shadow of their lives apart again. Not once did they think to offer their names.

Helen Iles.

Binary Wave

In summer, my shoulders glint
in the noonday sun. Magnifying
minnows in the shallows, filling sandcastle
moats, and draping tendrils
of mermaid hair. Conducting
sand orchestras, replenishing rockpools,
and pushing children
towards frozen treats. I am why
you always return
to the beach.

In winter, my shoulders glare
a shade of dusk. Bashing
lighthouse windows, knocking ships
off course, and dragging sailors
to the depths. Escorting sharks
to the shore, beaching dolphins,
and pushing towns
off the map. I am why
you never turn your back
on the ocean.

Kathleen Knight

They Wait

After invasion
still comes welcome
to Country. They wait
for acknowledgement
on Country. They wait
for *dadirri,* for lore,
for kinship
to make sense
for the newcomers. They wait.

After invasion
still comes ceremony
on Country. They wait
for recognition
on Country. They wait
for a message stick, for songlines,
for sacred sites
to make sense
for the newcomers. They wait.

After invasion
still comes welcome
and ceremony
while they wait.

Kathleen Knight

Her Own Woman

Observation Profile

The woman at the table opposite mine, long, grey hair constrained by a black ribbon, holds a piece of blue material in one hand. Seated on a smallish plastic chair, brown slacks, a snug beige top, white sandals, she seems to spread in all directions. Grimacing, face flushed, she leans forward over the Singer sewing machine standing on the work surface in front of her. Movement is awkward but the fingers that pin the paper pattern to the material are nimble, practised. Scissors, sourced from a transparent green plastic container at her side, slice around the pattern. Pins removed, she slides the material under the needle, pushes down the guard, works the treadle. The Singer whirs as she works.

Four others trail in. Unpacking a variety of handiwork, settling along the table, they talk amongst themselves. The low-level hum of their conversation signals that this is a library. A large white card, *Crafters' Circle, Wednesday, 1.30-4.30*, explains.

One of the four leans across. Squinting, she picks up the packet containing patterns. "Old fashioned," she says, indicating the brightly coloured illustration of three dolls in different dresses. "Kids won't want these. They'll want Anna and Elsa – you know, that Disney film."

Behind the sewing machine, the woman shrugs, expressionless. "These are my generation and my granddaughter just loves that I make them for her."

The critic tosses the packet, takes up a crochet needle and a ball of red wool.

Ignoring her, the woman is busy again, this time trimming loose threads.

The Singer roars now and time passes. The others pack up, do their leave-taking. She bobs her head, doesn't look up. The foot on the treadle slips out of its sandal. She grunts, then holds up a tiny blue dress. I clap my hands appreciatively. She looks across in surprise, smiling as she packs the new outfit reverently into the container.

A glance then towards the exit: "They talk too much," she says scathingly. "I just come to do the work."

I nod but I'm puzzled. Why join a circle if she doesn't want to chat? Then I remember the negative comment made by the crafter with the crochet needle. Maybe negativity is a feature of this group and she keeps hoping someone like herself, whose focus is on the crafting, will join.

I'm here to observe, not to speculate, but I can't help wondering if she'll be back next week.

Marilyn Rainier

Stained

In England, we didn't call them hobby farms but that was what they were. Ours was called Goose Farm, although somewhere in those early years I learnt that its original name had been Gorse Farm. This was due to the gorse bushes which grew, intertwined with blackberry and hawthorn, along the hedgerows.

'The lower orders,' my father would say, 'have a problem with the Doric 'r' – 'and he would give his listener the local Kentish rendering of the word 'gorse' in explanation.

My parents had a black lacquered double bed which bore the legend 'By Appointment to His Majesty the King'. This was painted on its headboard, in gold lettering. I therefore had no difficulty identifying my father with royalty, although my mother, who spent most of her time with the hired help in the kitchen, never seemed to fall into this category.

Goose Farm, together with the surrounding properties, was owned by my grandmother. The farm provided her with many hectares of fields and woodlands on which to ride and graze her horses. She always rode side saddle, in long brown skirt and jacket, a matching hard hat almost covering the tightly netted chignon.

I can see her now, a small, erect figure, brushing aside the leafy overhang with the short crop she invariably held in her right hand, my half-sister, Louisa, riding American cross saddle, a little way behind her. Beside them, their numbers varying from two to four, ran the dogs.

My father had been married before. He favoured driving a

vintage Bentley at speed on country excursions and, on a particularly rough road, the pin holding the passenger door snapped. His wife was thrown out and died instantly. Louisa, who was at this time only six months old, went to live with my grandmother in what could only be described as a Gothic mansion that served as a hunting lodge situated at the other end of the estate. Six months later, my father met and married my mother and brought her to live on the farm.

I was told I was a pre-term baby. Lucky to survive, they said, often with pursed lips and a perplexing shake of the head that I could never decode. My mother told me of my father's disappointment that I was not the eagerly anticipated son. The florist delivered a single bouquet. So, there was me – and eighteen months later there was Charles. This time my mother was concerned about too much pollen.

Louisa and Charles had little love for one another but shared the freedom of knowing that, if I was with them, they could do what they wished, then blame me, and I would suffer the consequences. I developed the habit of eating breakfast early and disappearing into the woods for hours, or hiding in the summerhouse with a book.

Schooldays were more difficult, as Louisa shared a string of governesses with Charles and myself. 'Unsuitable' was the word used as each packed and left. Mademoiselle Paillot, whom my father finally produced as a fitting educator for us, appeared after one of his visits to France to study the language. Mademoiselle was a young woman with an excitable temperament who, to my distress, seemed to lose no opportunity to speak ill of my beloved mother – although never in her presence. Her passion for *marons glaces* meant her touch was often sticky, as was my father's after her arrival, which puzzled me as he expressed a dislike for these sweets. I detested my governess's cold embrace and sharp tongue but any attempts to escape her in my grandmother's large garden and surrounding paddocks were thwarted by the arrival of her dog, Toby. A foul-breathed wire-haired terrier, gifted to Mademoiselle by my grandmother, it seemed to make a point of tracking me down when I sought secret retreats under the hedges in my grandmother's garden.

Although my grandmother kept horses, she did not enjoy their company as she enjoyed the company of her dogs. She spoke often of their pedigrees and at night time had them enclosed in a yard in the inner sanctum of the house. As a hunting lodge, the house had been designed to accommodate not only the hunters but the hounds that accompanied the hunt.

My grandmother never had less than a dozen dogs in the house and during the Second World War. She also accommodated the pack of fox hounds which ran with our local hunt. To keep these hounds from attacking her own dogs, she had kennels built behind the box hedge separating the gardens and lawns from the vegetable garden. These kennels, originally painted white but now streaked with green lichens, were foul-smelling and damp. It was my grandmother's pleasure to lock me in one or other of them when reports of my misbehaviour reached her. Louisa and Charles would taunt me through the wire netting.

Once a month, my father would escort my grandmother, Mademoiselle, Louisa and Charles on a shopping trip to London, some forty miles away. They would leave first thing in the morning, returning late in the afternoon. I stayed home, at my mother's request, to keep her company and it was on these days that we would share a secret freedom. In spring and summer, we would pack a picnic and go looking for violets and primrose in the woods. We would laugh and sing and fill a basket with wildflowers. In autumn, we gathered hazelnuts and blackberries; in winter, shiny-leafed holly with its scarlet berries and chestnuts to roast on the fire.

My father never hit my mother but lashed her instead with his tongue. He seemed to take pleasure in humiliating her in front of the servants, and Mademoiselle in particular. Her rebellion was to eat and she grew massive, a factor which only added fuel to my father's taunts.

We stayed in the woods for as long as we dared. Sensing my mother's sometimes overwhelming sadness, I became an expert mimic and would be rewarded by her calls for repeat performances.

'Mademoiselle again,' she would cry from her seat under a shady tree, and I would oblige. My reward was the tears of laughter on her plump, pretty face. Sometimes she looked so young, so vulnerable, and my heart would ache as we walked home together.

The day when the end began was the first day of the holidays. The last week of school had, for me, been unusually peaceful, for Mademoiselle had lost her dog, Toby. The terrier spent its days stretched out on the sofa in the school room and had a habit of lifting its leg against our desks. Louisa and Charles found this funny but for me, this added to my sense of the place being somehow rotten and oppressive. Mademoiselle would, with glace powdered pout, remonstrate with the little dog, then gather him to her and forgive him by burying her blonde head in his brown and white curls.

Despite the servants' best efforts, the smell of dog urine, mixed with disinfectant, permeated our schoolroom, as it did the passageway from the courtyard behind the kitchen, along which my grandmother's dogs ran at exercise time. A gardener was employed whose main task was to clean up after the dogs and, when Toby disappeared, I suspected that this old man, whose arthritic frame moved painfully slowly, had failed to close the gate to the vegetable garden. This was my suspicion but I kept my counsel.

Mademoiselle set work for us and spent several days scouring the hedgerows. My grandmother, whose austerity did not stretch to dogs, allocated her a farm labourer to assist with the search. Toby did not reappear and my father, showing unusual kindness, drove Mademoiselle down to Brighton for some sea air to help her recover from her loss.

On this first day, then, I awoke early and packed a sandwich and a drink in the rectangular lunch box my mother had given me for my forays. It was her way of showing me she understood. With a full day ahead, I planned hours of uninterrupted reading in the silence of the woods.

Clearing away the traces of my breakfast, I slipped into the garden and picked a newly opened pink rose, placing it on the breakfast table for my mother. Placing my lunch box and my book in my shoulder bag, I closed the door quietly, ran down the front path, and out across the laneway. The field ahead of me, still veiled in morning mist, led to the opening to the woods.

This field was named Pink Field because of the reddish clay that was turned up there during ploughing. Each area of the farm had its own name and the farm worker who was instructed to, "Turn the cows out on the Rolling Banks", or "Get the mare out of Colonel's field and take her for shoeing,' knew exactly where he was going. Only men worked on the land. Both my grandmother and my father had strong ideas about a woman's place, although it was tacitly understood that my grandmother's wealth exempted her from the restraints placed upon other women.

As I crossed Pink Field and entered the woods, the trees closed together above me and for a moment it was dark. Then, as I squeezed my eyes to slits, the pale magic of the place settled about me and I looked ahead at the sea of blue which gave its name to this corner of the farm – the Bluebell Woods. I stood for a moment, ecstatic, feeling the wonder, as I always did, of such a carpet. Then I began to make my way along the footpath towards Big Pond, where my father kept his boat.

There were two ponds in the woods. Little Pond was overhung by pine trees and, at this time of year, so enclosed by bracken that trying to reach it was no pleasure. Big Pond, situated in a clearing in the woods, was banked by rhododendrons and almost bracken-free. It was covered in summertime with a round-leafed green weed but the weed had shallow roots and never clogged up the paddle wheels in the boat as some weeds could. I planned to lie in the boat and read.

The boat that lay moored at the edge of Big Pond was old and little used. My father had brought it to the farm on a whim and soon tired of it. It had a wooden seat across the centre and one at each end. I clambered in, placed my lunch on the centre seat, and began to clear out the tree branches and leaves that had fallen into it since my last visit.

As I pushed my hands under the right-hand seat, I felt something hard. I pulled out a small pair of blue secateurs which were beginning to show signs of rust. I looked at them in astonishment. They were my mother's; the pair she used to cut flowers for the house. I was warmed by the thought of her pleasure when I returned them to her. I placed them beside me while I read.

The sun shone warmly and the hours passed quickly. Soon it was lunchtime and I decided to paddle to the middle of the pond so I could watch the frogs and other pond life through the weeds as I ate my sandwich. I leaned forward to turn the paddle handles but they did not move. Surprised, I pulled the handles backwards. Still nothing. The water was too deep for the paddles to be jammed in the mud. I climbed out of the boat and began to pull on the long mooring line.

It moved slowly upwards and, as the paddle wheels rose higher, I saw that one of them had run foul of some sacking.

Taking off my shoes and socks, I waded in and pulled at the hessian. It moved up slowly from the bottom of the pond. It was not a piece of sacking, I saw, but a sack with something inside it. Carefully, I pulled the soggy, fibrous material out and away from the paddle and slid my hand down to separate it from its holding. It was bulky and refused to move. I saw now that there was twine tied around the top of the sack. The end of it must have wound itself around the inside of the wheel. I returned to the boat and picked up the secateurs. Leaning over the edge, I lifted the sack and cut the twine. The hessian left its jammed space and I lifted it into the boat.

Cutting the neck of the wet sacking, I pulled it open and looked down at what was inside. A smell of rotting flesh, mixed with the dampness of the sacking, reached me. Short, curly, hair, brown and white. I had found Mademoiselle's beloved dog. I had found Toby. Nauseated, I stood up and flung the sack away from me onto the bank, where it thudded and lay still just above the waterline.

Shivering, I crouched in the bottom of the boat, staring at the secateurs I held in my hand. My mind raced in search of an explanation. Secateurs were easy to come by. Maybe these didn't, after all, belong to my mother. Perhaps Toby had been caught in a rabbit trap and the farm labourer who set the traps, fearing my grandmother's anger, had counted on the water rotting the evidence. Maybe these were his secateurs; just a coincidence…

I must have sat there for some time, hunched in the bottom of that boat. My heart was racing and I was afraid. Then I remembered a story I had read where a body had been thrown into a lake in a sack weighted down by rocks. The body hadn't been discovered until the murderer had died years later, leaving a note.

I climbed quickly out of the boat and jumped onto the bank, careful to avoid the sack. I tied up the boat, then began to search amongst the knotted trunks and low-lying, cool dark leaves of the rhododendrons. Soon I had collected a pile of bulky, misshapen rocks. It was heavy work but I didn't dare to stop until I had piled them, one by one, in the bottom of the boat.

Gingerly, then, I caught the sack by the neck and dragged it into the water. Struggling with the weight and its awkwardness, I climbed into the boat and pulled it up behind me. Red-stained water oozed onto the floor of the boat and I bit my lip as I centred myself on the slatted wooden seat and gripped the handles, my feet jammed against the rocks.

With the added weight, the boat lay dangerously low in the water but, as I pushed, the familiar clunk clunk of the paddles began and the boat moved slowly out and away from the bank. I looked behind me. Water and weed sluiced up through the paddle wheels but all around was emptiness.

My thin wrists hurt and it seems to take forever but now I am at the centre, where the water is deepest. I pull my blouse up by the neck, across my nose and mouth. I don't want to be sick and, as I open the neck of the sack. I look away as I thrust each stone into the rottenness.

Soon they are all in. I gather up the shortened strands of twine and twist them into the tight, double knot that I use to secure my lace-up shoes. I heave the sacking onto the edge of the boat, then shut my eyes and push hard. There is a splash. The small craft rocks and heaves upwards. I open my eyes and watch, fascinated, as the green web of weed closes over the foul-smelling stained receptacle. Now all is silent but the taste for adventure has left me and I rinse my hands carefully, remove the drink bottle from my lunch box, and replace it with the secateurs. Pushing the drink bottle into my pocket, I dry my hands on my handkerchief, then reach again for the handles.

My mother was in the kitchen, slicing vegetables for the evening meal. She always insisted on doing the cooking herself.

She smiled as I walked in.

'You must be hungry. I've made a cake.'

I shook my head and pushed the lunch box across the table, lifting the lid as I did so.

'These. Are they yours?'

Nothing had prepared me for the way her face crumpled. I watched as she raised a hand to her mouth and began to run her thumbnail slowly backwards and forwards across her bottom teeth. I'd noticed this habit before. She did it when my father was lashing her with cruel words. I couldn't bear to think that something I had done was causing her to look like that; to be so unhappy.

Her eyes were of a particularly vivid blue. Now they stared vacantly at the secateurs. She put her hands behind her back.

'Poor Toby,' she whispered. Then she looked across at me. The blue eyes had no centres. 'Accidents happen,' she said softly.

I nodded, withdrawing the lunch box.

'They're a bit rusty. I'll sandpaper them for you.'

'You'll do it yourself?' The gaze was steady.

'Yes – just me.' I closed the lid. She smiled quickly and reached for the cake tin. I didn't question her silence. She was helpless in a way I couldn't understand.

Early in July, there was another upset at my grandmother's house. Dan, the large Airedale my grandmother prized because he ran beside her when she went horse riding, was missing. The local police were notified but the dog was not to be found. My grandmother was at her dourest and I was careful to stay quietly in the school room, avoiding the gardens where the search was centred. When my mother was out shopping one morning, I checked the kitchen drawers. The secateurs, now shiny from my sandpapering, were still there. Relieved, I closed the drawer tightly.

In September, it was Clou's turn. Clou was a White West

Highland terrier. My grandmother said Clou was Gaelic for 'small'. He slept in her bedroom with her.

This time, the police took the situation seriously. The dogs, all pedigrees, were valuable. Obviously, someone was stealing them. Had we seen or heard anything suspicious?

The farm workers were nervous. They knew my grandmother. Ray Jones, the ploughman, a man of fifty-odd, was found to have a minor record for theft as a teenager. He supported his elderly parents. He pleaded with my father. I could have told him to save his words.

A week before Christmas, I decided to surprise my mother by collecting the chestnuts she would need for the turkey stuffing. Louisa and Charles were working on a version of the Nativity play. I was the innkeeper. I recited my lines quickly and told them I was going for a walk.

'To those old woods again!' Charles groaned. 'Why can't you help us with the stage set?'

'I'll bring you some chestnuts."

He shrugged and turned back to his work but he loved chestnuts. I knew now he would defend me if Louisa complained that I hadn't helped with the play.

From my grandmother's house, I had to cross several fields in order to reach the end of the woods but I knew a copse where the chestnuts were thick on the ground. I took gloves and a shoulder bag. The prickly chestnut casings would be better opened at home. The ground was covered in a thin layer of snow and the sky was black with more snow clouds. I would have to move quickly.

Soon there was only one more field between me and the chestnut copse. The field was ploughed and the chilled furrows were hard under my feet. When I finally reached the heavy wooden gate on the other side, my hands were too cold to pull back the metal catch that secured it. First kneeling, then flattening myself against the ground, I was able to slip carefully under the electric fence that bounded the woods. My breath made small clouds in the air as I scrambled to my feet. Hugging myself to keep warm and a little out of breath I began to make my way through the dead, brown bracken. There was a crack of twigs ahead and I started as a red fox ran through the trees.

Now I was on the footpath. As I looked, I could see the chestnut trees, taller than the surrounding woods, up ahead. I pulled my balaclava down and tucked it into my coat collar. The top button came undone. I stopped to fasten it. Again a twig cracked. A rabbit? Another fox? Quietly, keeping close to the trees, I moved towards the sound.

Through the bracken, I caught a glimpse of someone pushing into the thicker woods. I sighed in disappointment as I saw it was my mother, carrying a swollen bag that she had obviously already filled. She, too, knew where the chestnuts lay thickest, and seeing me occupied with the nativity play she had obviously decided to come here alone. My only thought now was to help her. I pushed quickly through the undergrowth and emerged beside her. With a start, she released the bag she was carrying. It slumped to the ground. Ashen-faced, she stared at me.

'You! You were at rehearsal!'

She moved in front of the bag but it was too late. I found myself staring at it in horror. The canvas was marked with red-brown stains.

'Chestnuts,' I whispered, filled with the dread of what I knew. 'I came to collect chestnuts – for you.'

For a moment the vivid blue stare, then she looked away.

'That's good of you. Really kind. I'll just get rid of this, then we'll collect them together.'

Biting back my fear, I looked at the bag.

'Would you like me to help?'

She nodded.

'Yes, that's an idea. You know this place better than I do.' She smiled at me, then shivered and pulled her coat around her. I wanted to take her hands, to reassure her.

'The chestnut trees. They're big. There are hollows inside the roots where …' My mouth was dry. '… it'll be softer for digging.' She nodded.

'You go ahead. I'll follow you.'

She picked up the bag. It hung between us. Sickened, I wanted to turn away. The snow clouds were oppressive now, seeming almost to touch the tops of the trees.

'Do you want me to carry it for you?' I asked quietly.

She nodded, the blue stare unseeing.

I placed the strap across my shoulder and swung the bag behind me.

'Those are the best ones. See. They're close together.' I motioned towards a clump of trees to our right. 'There's an old fox earth under the one in the middle. We can hollow it out.'

Turning away from her, I began to push through the undergrowth. I didn't want to look, didn't want to see the stain which I knew must now be soaking through my coat. Shrubs and small trees forced me to bend. There was a clearing ahead. I made towards it.

I didn't mean to cry out, didn't mean to frighten her, but they moved so quickly from behind the trees. There were two of them. They stood in front of me, barring my way, the dark blue of their uniforms standing out starkly against the brown of the winter bracken. I don't know which of them spoke. Maybe both.

'We'll take that if you don't mind.'

Hands reached out for the bag.

'No!' I screamed.

I turned around. But my mother was no longer there.

Marilyn Rainier

Anatomy of an Accident

11.58 pm:

The Tuart had been a sapling when the newcomers arrived. Unlike the original wayfarers, these vicious creatures chopped and sawed its companions down one by one, while its roots cringed in empathy at their pain. Others were destroyed by noxious, noisy machinery and heavy chains. Now the mature Tuart stood alone beside the creek that flowed only after winter rains.

A walking trail crossed the creek where the original wayfarers passed on their journeys. After the newcomers arrived, the trail was widened to a track, then a road. A bridge was built, first in timber and later in concrete, while the road above widened further and gained a hard black top.

For eighty years the Tuart watched the progress impassively, unaffected by these new arrivals. Until the time their metal contraptions began roaring and flashing by, faster than the swiftest bird. The impacts commenced when the metal machines failed to negotiate the bend before the bridge. It was the occasional collision at first; a thump into its trunk that dislodged a piece of bark and shook its lower branches. Over the years the velocity of the impacts grew, along with the resulting scars on its slowly increasing girth.

Tonight, it had happened again; this one the most violent of all. The force of the impact speared the vehicle upwards and sideways, gouging a groove across the Tuart's trunk and smashing into its lowest branch so forcefully the timber splintered. Now the ancient limb hung, shattered and bleeding, an open wound for voracious beetles so long denied entry to its aging body.

After a pause, numerous vehicles arrived at the scene, lights blazing and sirens blaring, disturbing the peaceful evening. They recovered their metal compatriot and its dislodged creatures, and departed. The Tuart shook its leaves in impotent frustration as it settled back into the quiet country night.

8.23 pm:

Brianna Outlander was surprised when, after a few miles exceeding the speed limit by she dared not think how much, the green sports car slowed and slewed into a side street on two wheels. Seven of the eight occupants cheered. The driver piloted the car around a few more bends and corners, seeming to know the route, and then at a dead end, spun the car in a circle – twice – tyres screaming in smoky protest.

Someone in the back seat said, "That'll stir up your old man, for sure!"

Brianna leaned across the girl next to her and asked her cousin, Kasye Coad, "Who's he talking about?"

Kasye grunted, Brianna was unsure whether in reply to her question or the g-forces the spinning car was imparting on its occupants. After the car straightened, she said, "Hayds' old man. He's a cop."

Brianna gasped, and grabbed the door handle as the car careened around another corner and through a roundabout as the driver returned to the highway.

A short while later another girl said, so quietly Brianna thought no one else had heard, "I feel sick."

Apparently, a girl in the back seat *had* heard, because she called, "Hey, Hayds! Can you drop us off at Macca's, mate? I need a smoke."

The driver replied, "Sure, Sue. Had enough already? Can't take the heat, eh?"

Most of the others laughed.

The car entered the McDonald's car park relatively slowly. As Brianna tumbled out, allowing the other girl to escape, she thought about remaining at McDonald's. But how could she keep an eye on her cousin if she left the car?

With much shuffling of bodies, two people, a young man and the girl who had spoken, climbed from the rear of the sports car, leaving one couple in the back. They made it quite clear they did not want Brianna cramping their action, so she climbed back in the front.

Perhaps it was habit that made her reach for the seat belt.

"Hey, what are you doing?" her cousin protested. "You don't need that! No way am I going to sit on a bloody seat buckle all night."

The driver shuffled over slightly. "Right, babes. Ready for a little action? Let's test this thing out, see who we can shake up."

"Let's go, Hayds!" Kasye gave an enthusiastic yell.

Brianna gripped the door handle.

7.56 pm:

Vivian Coad pulled away from the kerb suppressing a sense of foreboding. She didn't trust her sister's child, perhaps a result of never quite trusting her sister when they were teens. They had grown up in Perth, but her sister now lived in Geraldton, a wild, outlaw frontier if the newspapers were to be believed.

She glanced in the rear-view mirror, but the girls had already entered the picture theatre. Heaving an uncertain sigh, she told herself they couldn't get into too much trouble inside the theatre. Anyway, with Kasye now dating a policeman's son, she expected he would be well-behaved, respectable and responsible.

If anything happened to Kasye tonight, she would hold her daughter's cousin responsible. Brianna Outlander was two years older than Kasye; almost an adult and surely mature enough to be held responsible for her actions. In the past few months when Vivian had trusted her daughter alone at the theatre on Saturday nights, nothing had happened. If that changed, she would definitely hold Brianna responsible.

8.06 pm:

Eight teenagers had crammed into the two-door sports car. Brianna wondered how the driver could, well, drive, squashed against the door like he was. And no one was wearing a seat belt. Impossible, she guessed, to decide who would miss out – or perhaps share. Four had squeezed into the back designed to seat only two comfortably. She was jammed against the passenger-side door, with Kasye and another girl between her and the driver.

"Let's see what this heap of overpriced crap can do!" yelled a male from the back seat.

Shouts of agreement accompanied his challenge and the car shot from the kerb like the proverbial bullet; engine screaming, tyres squealing and black rubber marking their route from the kerb outside the cinema. The car snaked down the road and slowed as the driver fought for, and regained control.

Just as Brianna dared an intake of breath, the car sped up again. It shot through a red light, to her horror and everyone else's – it seemed – delight, judging by their squeals and screams and yells of encouragement.

8.29 pm:

The squeal of tyres and smell of burning rubber had Sergeant Harrison leaping from the bed before he was fully awake. "Bloody hoons! I'll catch those louts if it's the last thing I do!"

"You won't catch them dressed like that," his wife said mildly from their double bed. She was still awake, reading with a booklight so her husband could sleep undisturbed. Fat chance on a Saturday night, she thought, bracing for his usual rant.

"Bloody irresponsible parents! That's who I blame. Why they can't keep their kids in line, I want to know. Should know where they are at all times, like we do."

"Yes dear," she murmured when he paused for breath. She'd tried arguing and reasoning with him in the past and knew the futility of it. These days she didn't bother to contradict him. She watched him pull his dressing gown from the wardrobe and fling it around his nakedness. A moment later the front door slammed. She turned back to her book. The hoons would be already gone. She thought about checking that their son Haydn, 'Hayds' to his mates, was indeed in his room. Earlier tonight she'd tried his door, but it was locked. It was usually locked lately. She hadn't knocked, although his light was on. Teenagers deserved some respect and privacy.

7.54 pm:

"Thanks, Auntie Viv," Brianna farewelled her mother's sister. She stepped backwards, onto the kerb, watched the car pull away and turned to follow her younger cousin and into the cinema.

Inside, she looked around for Kasye.

"Pssst!"

Brianna spun around. "Kase! What...?" Her cousin was standing at the doorway to the Ladies toilets, frantically beckoning her.

"Inside," Kasye hissed and flounced away.

Mystified, Brianna followed. "What gives?" she asked after the outer door had closed behind them.

"You didn't actually think we came here to watch some dumb movie?" Kasye scoffed.

"Then why *are* we here?" Brianna felt a cold chill ripple through her body. Had her cousin as good as called her a party pooper? Did Auntie Viv have good reason to question her daughter's interest in movies, even after Kasye's spiel about the machinations of moviedom and the finer points of filming?

Kasye rolled her eyes. "To fool mum, of course. You're not going to squeal on me, are you?"

"Why do you need to fool her?"

"You'll understand when you meet the others."

"Who? How many?"

Kasye shrugged. "Depends who turns up." She turned to Brianna and grasped her arm. "Look, you're welcome to go in and watch the movie, if you don't think you can keep quiet."

Instinct told Brianna it would be the wiser move, but curiosity drew her in. "It's okay," she said, "I'll go with you."

9.52 pm:

"Looks like they've given up," Kasye said. "I can't see any coloured lights flashing behind us now."

Brianna felt she could take a breath for perhaps the second time that night. The police had been chasing them for what seemed like hours. Along highways, through too many red lights to count, the wrong way down the freeway just because Hayds wanted to give them a thrill – her and Kasye or the police, Brianna didn't ask – and now they were speeding along some obscure country road. She supposed she should be grateful it was still bitumen.

"The pigs never give up. They've probably got a chopper upstairs," said the male in the back seat.

Brianna glanced over her shoulder. She couldn't see much, but the couple seemed to be sitting upright now. The last time she'd looked, they were horizontal. She hadn't looked too closely and decided not to think what they might be up to.

"Or be waiting in the next town," Kasye added.

Brianna thought her city cousin didn't sound so cheerful now. Had she had enough excitement?

Suddenly the car swerved across the road and back, throwing Brianna against the door and then against her cousin.

"Hey, stop that!" Kasye yelped.

"Stop what?" Hayds said and swung the wheel again, more violently this time. The car fishtailed down the empty road, tossing all three in the front seat from side to side like half-inflated bouncy balls.

When the car was steering in a straight line again, Hayds said irritably, "Hey, babe! Don't ever knock my arm like that again! I know you can't keep your hands off me, but I'm trying to steer this thing."

"And don't hit me!" Kasye yelled, slapping his face.

Brianna wondered if he had slapped her first and she hadn't seen it. Then Kasye's body jerked against hers from Haydn's fist, swung backwards from the steering wheel, striking her face, delivered with all the force he could muster in the restricted space. Kasye's hands flew to her face as she screamed, ironically muffling the sound.

"Cut it out, you two," said the male in the back seat.

Brianna wondered if his girlfriend was capable of speech. So far she'd not spoken.

The car sped up again.

The girl in the back seat screamed.

"The bridge!" yelled the male. "Slow down!"

Brianna looked ahead. Where the road curved away, behind a small bridge barrier a huge tree trunk almost filled the windscreen...

Shirley Rowland

The Engagement Party

Saturday, 8 29 am:

"'Morning, Grandpop," Justine says when she enters the kitchen and sees him talking to her mother.

"You're up late," her mother, hands immersed in a sudsy sink, says.

"Keeping out of the way, Mum. I know how busy you are today."

"And when is your big day planned, love?" her grandfather asks.

"There's not going to be one, Grandpop."

"Oh? It's traditional for the oldest to marry first. You should be getting engaged before your sister."

"Not this time, Grandpop. I've decided I'm not getting married, ever. But I don't see why that should stop Olivia and Max."

"You disappoint me, Justine. What about your future? Who will look after you when your parents are gone?"

"I'm perfectly capable of looking after myself. Being independent. Women can do anything nowadays." She turns to leave the room.

Her mother asks, "Where are you going?"

"I've decided I'm not hungry after all, Mum. See you later, Grandpop." She dashes back to her bedroom before anyone can see how much her body is shaking.

The party is in full swing. More than sixty people have gathered on the back lawn, an area that could easily accommodate three times the number. Isaac 'Ike' Mulligan stands at his back door watching them; older groups in animated discussion, younger ones dancing to raucous music blaring from speakers placed at strategic corners of the mown grass.

He looks past them and admires the spring flush of new pink and copper leaves on the trees surrounding the lawn, inhales the scent of flowering creepers garnishing the fenced pool competing with the heady eucalypt odours from the flowering gums and bottlebrushes, and decides his semi-rural acreage has never looked so lush.

Closer to the house, a catering tent holds the remains of the afternoon's gourmet offerings. Ike is debating whether to search its half-melted ice chests for an unopened bottle of wine when an older man greets him.

"Good party, Ike. Although one thing disappoints me."

Ike turns to his guest. He knows what his father-in-law is about to say, but feels obliged to ask anyway. "And what is that, Noah?"

"I would have expected your eldest daughter, Justine, to be the first to celebrate an engagement."

"In this day and age, they make their own decisions," Ike says with deceptive mildness.

"You're not tough enough on your daughters. It's the father's job to find them suitable husbands, starting with the oldest. Yet Olivia's your middle girl."

"Times have changed, Noah."

"I hope you've carefully vetted the young man."

"He works for me."

"Employ them. Very sensible. But what about Justine?"

"What about her?"

"No prospects? I thought she was in a steady relationship?"

"As I said, Noah, they make their own decisions." He sighs in relief when he sees his wife, Brenda, walking towards them.

"Move aside Ike, Dad. The cake's finally arrived."

"Not before time," Ike says, not because he's concerned about the cake, but to escape his father-in-law's outdated opinions. He steps aside; admires the care with which the caterers carry a three-tier cake towards the tent.

"Ready, dear?" Brenda says, distracting him.

He turns and takes her hand. Casually he wonders how she managed to organise perfect spring weather to complement the buzzing party.

"As I'll ever be," he says with a wry smile. She squeezes his hand and leads them to the table where the caterers have deposited the cake. His eyebrows rise at the white icing decorated with black spots and lines and random letters. Only the topmost layer has readable words – sort of. *Happy Engagement, Olz & Max.*

Beside him, Brenda says, "At least it's not black and covered in skulls and crossbones. That was my greatest fear."

"But Olz?"

Her manicured face scrunches. "You know them. The Zed Force. Since primary school." She shrugs. "It could be worse."

"In so many ways," he ends for her.

On cue, the happy couple emerge from the crowd, holding hands and laughing. Ike frowns at their clothing choices, but then forces a smile. Olivia, 'Olz', is swathed in white frills as if already walking down the aisle, and tottering on six-inch stilettos. He shudders at the damage they must be inflicting on the lawn. Max is wearing a shirt with a collar. In the two years Max has been his employee, Ike has never seen him wear anything more formal than a T-shirt.

A murmur ripples through the crowd as they sense the cake-cutting ceremony is about to commence, and merge into a semi-circle behind the guests of honour.

Five Days Earlier, 8.07 am:

Justine remains in her room until she hears her father's car engine fading into the distance. She has already excused herself from the usual Monday morning rush as her father and sister prepare for work and her youngest sister for school.

Knowing her mother will now be alone in the kitchen, Justine enters. "Mum, are you busy?" she asks, already knowing the answer.

"What do you think?" her mother replies irritably. "Why are you still home? Don't you have work today?"

"I've decided to call in sick." Justine suppresses a smile as she watches her mother's eyebrows rise. *That surprised you. I knew it would.*

"Are you unwell? What's wrong?" Her mother groans. "The last thing I need this week is a sick child."

"Mum, I'm not sick and I'm not a child!" Justine takes a deep breath to control her irritation and notices her mother doing likewise.

"Then why are you here?"

"To talk to you. Woman to woman."

"You're not going to cause trouble at your sister's party, are you?"

"No, Mum. Although it *is* what I want to talk to you about."

"Then start talking. I've got a lot to do and no time to do it all."

"I've been thinking all weekend and I've reached a decision."

"Go on."

"You know how Grandpop keeps rabbiting on about the oldest girl marrying first, in the tradition of his 'old country.' It might have worked for him and Nana, but this is the twenty-first

Century. It's not going to work for us, especially with Olz' engagement party next Saturday. *And,*" Justine hurries on as she sees her mother raise a hand, "I've heard you and Dad arguing about it when you think we girls can't hear. So, I've decided," she pauses for emphasis, "I'm not going to get married. Ever. So Olivia and Penny are free to do it if and when they want to."

She waits a moment for her mother's reaction, knowing how much influence her grandfather has over his only daughter. "There. I've said it. Marriage is a con. Expecting some man to take care of me when I'm perfectly capable of taking care of myself."

"But you and Eric?"

"Have busted up. I'm not going to stand in the way of my sister's happiness. As far as I'm concerned, she and Max can marry tomorrow if they wish. I don't want me being oldest to stop them." She takes a breath and braces for her mother's reaction.

"Your grandfather will be furious."

"Tough. I'm not from his generation. The world has moved on."

"I dread telling him."

"Then I'll tell him."

"When?"

"Before the party starts. Don't worry, Mum, I'll make sure he understands it's not your doing."

Justine watches her mother collect the breakfast dishes from the table and begin to load the dishwasher, and then leaves to phone her boss.

One week Earlier, 9.05 pm:

Eric is surprised when Justine suggests they drive to the lookout on Monument Hill. Now they've arrived and he wonders what she wants to tell him. When she remains silent, he says, "What did you want to talk about, Justine?"

She waves her hand in a meaningless gesture. "Oh, this and that, you know."

He turns towards her. "No," he says, "I don't know." He watches her lift her shoulders and straighten her back, as if bracing for something unpleasant.

"It's Olivia and Max's engagement party next Saturday..." She stops.

"Max has already invited me, if that's what this is about."

"Oh no, it's not that!" Justine's chest heaves and her words tumble out in a rush. "It's just that I'm the oldest and I expected to become engaged and all the rest of it first. We've been going out for years, and I just, well, sort of expected..." She falters.

"And?" he prompts.

"I thought we could make it a double engagement. You and me. We could break it off later if you don't want... I mean..."

"Justine, I don't know what I've done to give you such an idea. If I've unwittingly led you on, I apologise, but I think the best way forward is to break up here and now – although I don't believe there is anything between us to break up."

She twists in her seat and gapes at him. "Just because I refused to go all the way once!"

He feels firmer ground now. "That has nothing to do with this. That move was a dare if you must know, which you quite rightly rejected. Probably got us both off the hook."

She makes a noise he can't quite identify but suspects it has something to do with crying. She starts struggling and he realises she's trying and failing to undo her seatbelt.

Suddenly it flies free and the buckle whacks the sidewall with a crash that makes him wince. The door flies open, almost snapping from its hinges, and she is outside standing in the dark.

He leans across. "Be sensible, Justine. It's too far to walk. Get back inside, I'll drive you home."

At first she doesn't move. Then she steps further away. After another long pause, she turns and starts walking towards the trees. Stumbles and almost falls. Walks into a spider's web, splutters and waves her arms frantically as she back-pedals.

He remembers her fear of spiders and waits. It's not long before she returns to his car, climbs in and closes the door. He wonders if the overwhelming relief he feels is some sort of crime as he leans forward to turn the ignition key.

11.58 pm:

Justine grinds her teeth and wonders if slashing her wrists would hurt any more than the emotional pain squeezing her chest. She wants to howl, let loose great wracking sobs to express the pain she feels. She tries to stop her mind from returning to the cause of that pain, skirt around the deep pit of despair inside which her anguish lies.

How could she have made such a gigantic blunder? Such a serious error of judgement? Such a monumental social gaff?

She slams her head into her pillow with such force her bed creaks. Her muscles freeze at the sound. Has Olivia heard it? The wall is brick. It should be soundproof, but comments her sister has made in the past causes Justine to control the volume of her grief now. *Damn Olivia! Does she know how much trouble she's caused me?*

Without warning, the deep pit opens up. Again she sees the silhouetted trees encircling the lookout like evil spectres. Their usual parking spot after the movies on a Saturday night. Its ages since Eric drove up here and tried to put a move on her. She assumes he's either shy or showing respect for her last rejection.

But she's changed her mind and hopes he'll try again. Not go all the way, of course. That would be irresponsible and reckless, and she's neither of those. But with Olivia's engagement party only a week away... Her three-years-younger sister has *her* life ahead mapped out. The future that she, Justine, expected to arrive at first. *How long should a girl hang out for 'Mr Right?' What if he never comes along? What might you miss out on by not accepting Mr Almost-right?*

So she told Eric she wanted to go to the lookout for old times' sake. Surely he took the hint when he agreed? The nightmare ignores her wish for oblivion and scrolls through her mind yet again. By the time it ends, she has made a decision.

Shirley Rowland

Contrasts

Cat, ginger in colour, sits,
like a speck
almost yellow
amidst the green

Sky, rich
foreboding turquoise
thundering blue
menacing glow
looms overhead

Little cat, dwarfed,
by the mighty sky
green sparkling grass
tipped with the gossamer,
of fallen rain

Stephanie Slanzi

Hospital food experience

Have you noticed how hospital food appeals to visitors more than to the patient? I have observed this at several hospitals over the past few months while visiting friends at Perth hospitals Fiona Stanley, Hollywood, Sir Charles Gairdner, the Mount, Murdoch, and St John's in Geraldton.

I have witnessed how the visitors are thrilled to share the food when offered by the patients. This especially applies to sweet things. The range of delectable morsels saved and distributed to visitors has included mini packets of biscuits, low-fat ice cream, pieces of fruit, cake, custard, and bread rolls.

This doesn't include the food patients receive from other visitors such as chocolates, grapes, mangoes, sweets, and biscuits which are also gobbled up by other visitors.

Perhaps the reason is patients are full from eating other food and leave their sweets. Or it could be their medication makes the sweets unappealing. Maybe some visitors time it perfectly by arriving at lunch or dinner time and their gracious and generous patient-host happily shares their treasures with them.

I hadn't realised the practice was so common until I accompanied people on hospital visits and saw daughters, sons, girlfriends, and friends, eagerly accepting and sharing the food on their visits.

Personally, I have savoured ice cream — although I feel guilty — until my friend welcomes me with a big smile and happily gives me her ice cream. Then I become one of the many visitors who share the hospital food experience.

Stephanie Slanzi

Time to fly

Time to fly she said as she dashed out the door
No time to talk about it now
The truth is she wanted to talk about it more
An offer she couldn't refuse

Congratulations on your new job Amy
You will enjoy the challenge
Glad you got this opportunity
An offer you couldn't refuse

Colleagues whip around with money and card
She is off to a new company
Why is leaving so hard?
For an offer too good to refuse

When it's time to leave the nest
The familiar people and places
Deep down we know it's for the best
To accept an offer she couldn't refuse

Stephanie Slanzi

A Visit to the Circus.

The three children – Eleanor, Julia and Alice – had not long returned from overseas where their father worked. Now they were back in England staying in their grandparents' house. It was a temporary arrangement, but they would be there for a couple of months and spending Christmas there too. Their father was home on leave and had taken extra time so there were other plans with places and people to visit later.

It was late in the year. Christmas was not far away and, being in the northern hemisphere, the days were drawing in. It was getting dark at four o'clock. The children had been out on an afternoon walk and were happy to be indoors again in the warmth. They were excited and told their grandmother about a poster they had seen picturing elephants and people dressed up with red noses and funny faces: Grandma told them these were clowns.

"Will we be able to go and see them properly?" asked Eleanor.

She had been reading a book by Enid Blyton about a circus and it sounded as though it would be wonderful to see a proper one instead of just reading about it. Her grandmother told them she had bought the tickets. When the circus arrived the following week, they would go to see it.

"Me too?" asked Alice. So often, being deemed too young, she stayed behind when her older sisters went on visits.

"Yes, dear, you are all going. Aunt Lily said she would be happy to take the three of you to the matinee. Mrs Galbraith and her daughter Moira will be going with you too."

They were excited and counted the days to the next Saturday. The day eventually arrived. The performance did not start till 3.30 so the street- lights were already on and the Big Top lit up. The circus was situated in the meadow at the edge of the town, not far from their grandmother's house. The children had been watching its arrival and the setting up of the main tent, or Big Top as it was called. There were caravans for the performers and cages for the animals. Elephants were not a novelty but there were other animals as well. Eleanor felt she knew all about circuses and told her sisters what she knew. Julia had not had a chance to read the book yet and was annoyed that her sister knew so much. Anyway, she was more interested in the horses that had arrived.

At last, it was time to go. They set off down the road with their aunt and followed the crowd through the gate to the entrance. Here Aunt Lily handed over the tickets. They had good seats right by the ring. Mrs Galbraith and Moira were already sitting there. The Galbraith family lived close by. Moira was the same age as Eleanor, and they had become good friends while the children were staying with their grandparents. Eleanor was looking forward to seeing the trapeze artists. Moira had shown her how to do handstands and cartwheels. Eleanor became quite proficient at these and had even tried "flying angels" off the swing in the garden.

The Circus ring itself had a thick layer of sawdust on it. They could see what they thought must be the trapeze ropes hooked up to the central poles. At last, the music and action started. First there was a parade of all the performers. Then various acts took place. Julia was fascinated by the horses and their riders. She had been having riding lessons and wondered if she could ever be able to stand on a horse's back and do what those girls were doing.

When the two clowns appeared, they mesmerised Alice. They

were so funny. One fell into a well. The other clown dropped a rope over the edge to pull him out. He had little success. So many different things came up on the rope. Where was the clown that had fallen in? A long string of flags came up and the clown looked round at the audience in despair, pulling up more rope with assorted items attached. By this time, Alice was laughing so much she wet her knickers and Aunt Lily took her outside. She never did find out what had happened to the clown in the well. Her sisters, being more interested in the horses and the performers on the trapeze, had dismissed the clowns as funny but not memorable.

The memory of the first circus seen as a four-year old had impressed Alice and lasted forever. No circus ever matched up to the enjoyment she remembered from that first visit. As an older person, when she took her own children to a circus, she found herself being critical as she could see the faults and the worn-out trappings of the set, and the clowns were not really funny at all. Her children enjoyed the experience though and she hoped they would keep happy memories too.

Alison P. Smith

Feeding a Toddler

Wine connoisseurs always examine their wine carefully before tasting it. They bring each sense into use. Sight. They hold the glass to the light looking for colour, and clarity, any cloudiness or unnecessary effervescence. Then the smell – any hint of corkage, acidity or just appreciating the bouquet as they twist the wine round the glass and sniffing and deciding on the fruitiness or any other aroma that may be present. The texture, if one could call it that, may be assessed by looking to see if there is any film left on the side of the glass. The connoisseurs do not roll the liquid between their fingers but would if it would in any way help them to decode the essence of the wine.

It is the same with the sense of hearing. A sparkling wine releases bubbles as it is poured into the glass. It does not snap, crackle and pop, but there is a soft ssss sound as the cork is removed. Are the bubbles too large or insufficient and flat? Care needs to be taken in pouring so that the wine does not bubble in a cascade over the edge of the glass. Then finally the taste. A small sip is taken and rolled around the mouth. If different wines are being tasted, this sip is spat out and another wine tried.

A toddler (for the purpose of this exercise the toddler is a boy) left with a plate of dinner will explore the proffered food in much the same way. He will look at the colour on the plate. It may just be a mixture but, if he is lucky, the foods will be separated. Orange mashed pumpkin or carrots, creamy white mashed potato, a bit of green – squashed peas, small broccoli florets or dark green puréed spinach – as well as something brown or white, either minced or flaked with a fork – lots of pretty colors arranged neatly in his bowl. He has been able to smell the dinner ever since his mother strapped him into his low chair with his plate in front of him. He is not sure if he is hungry or not. She has gone to answer the telephone and left him to feed himself for a few minutes.

The texture is important. Though his mother had put a small spoon in his hand he would rather use his fingers to feel the food. The small heap of mashed peas may have lumps and the creamed potato likewise. In this way, with his fingers, he explores the food in the dish. By the time he has finished doing that the plateful is now one swirling mass of the mixed colours and with his spoon he then digs in.

This is the next fun stage. Before putting anything into his mouth, he likes to test the viscosity. Will the food on the spoon stay there if he turns the spoon over? No, it falls off. What if he holds it over the edge of the feeding tray, what will happen then? Plop! It goes onto the floor. – interesting! It makes a flattened mess there. *If I were in a proper high-chair*, he thinks, *instead of this low one the food might make a bigger splash. It is time to try the taste. It is too late to taste each type of food by itself, but it looks interesting now that I have mixed it in the dish.*

He tries it. *Not bad*, he thinks, *but I don't like the lumpy bits. I will spit them out. I don't like the brown stuff either. The white stuff I had yesterday was easier to swallow. The brown stuff needs teeth and mine are still coming. The spoon is useless as the food doesn't stay on.*

As he turns the spoon to put it in his mouth, the food slides off. He uses his fingers instead and scoops up several mouthfuls. He finds he is hungry after all and eats most of what was there, except for the brown stuff and lumpy bits of vegetable. His mother comes back, the phone call took longer than she expected.

"Oh Tommy. What a mess you have made." She grabs a damp cloth and after taking off his bib wipes his face and hands then wipes down the food-tray that held the plate. "I will feed you the next course. You have spent enough time exploring your food." She puts stewed apples in a bowl with a spoonful of yoghurt on top and proceeds to feed him.

If Tommy could talk, he would tell you that he does not like someone feeding him. He likes to do it himself and prefers to assess the food and examine it first. He hates the way the spoon hovers in front of his face while he still has a mouthful. Sometimes he needs to bat away the hand that holds the spoon or turn his face away. He likes the mess he makes with his food, but Mummy never leaves him with it long enough. The creamy mashed potato would make a lovely castle and the mashed peas would be like the sea surrounding it. Daddy helped him make a sandcastle once when they went to the beach. Then sea came up and washed around it. That was fun. *You can squash jelly through your fingers if Mummy isn't looking or you can poke a large piece and see it wobble. There is so much you can do with food apart from eating it.*

Alison P. Smith.

Downsizing

Jim and Mary had been busy arranging the books onto the shelves. From time-to-time Jim would call her to ask what order he should put them in. They had recently moved to a smaller house. It was called down-sizing. The house certainly was much smaller than their previous one, but unfortunately, they had not had much success in downsizing their possessions. The books were a special problem.

They had packed the books in cardboard cartons and had labelled them, indicating the room the books had been in at the time of packing. This should have made it easier to decide where they should go. They had set aside several books to give to charity or to sell, but this did not seem to make much difference. Mary could not help but remember a time when they were first married and the few books they owned barely filled one shelf of a small bookcase. Now, fifty years later, they had a virtual library of their own.

In their previous large house, there were bookcases in every room. Mary had sorted the books – the non-fiction ones according to subject matter and the fiction ones into Australian authors and others (in alphabetical order of course). Biographies were also arranged together. Mary had at one time thought about being a librarian. It hadn't happened, but she prided herself on being able to find any book of theirs when required.

There were reference books in the office, art, and history, both natural and political in the dining room as well as language, plays and poetry. Various books of fiction, along with biographies were either in the living room or in the different bedrooms. There had still been a collection of children's books in what used to be the children's rooms. When the family had grown up and left home, they took their own books away, but there was still a good collection of children's classics which later the grandchildren had enjoyed. Mary was loath to give them away; some were part of her own childhood. Then there were craft books and a few cookery books which Mary had kept in their large kitchen.

There seemed hardly any space in the small kitchen of the new house. Mary only kept the cookery books in regular use in one small corner of the workbench, the remainder she had put away in a cupboard.

It was difficult. The bulk of the books were still in cartons. Mary wanted to go through them again before taking them to the Op-shop or second-hand bookshop. She was afraid something precious might have been overlooked in the packing. Jim tried to be helpful, but for much of the time he would browse through the books and then call out "You can't discard this one, I must read it again."

The books they wanted to keep were harder to arrange in their new place as the shelves were at different heights. This meant shelving by size rather than by subject matter or alphabetically. This upset Mary's sense of order.

They had thought they would be strong-minded and not buy any more books. Now they had moved to the township, they could borrow books regularly from the local library, or in desperation buy some from the second-hand shop which gave a small refund on returns, but this didn't work. The trouble with books and the enjoyment of reading, there was always another to borrow or buy.

At their time of life, friends or family often gave them bookshops vouchers for birthday or Christmas presents. This did not help the book problem and the new books became stacked on various surfaces.

Down-sizing was an impossible task.

Alison P. Smith

Pink and Sticky

I guess I have always been something of a conformist. I have never enjoyed "rocking the boat" and to do anything really wrong would really go against the grain.

With this in mind, people may think I have led a very dull life. Not so. My life has been great and I have enjoyed it all and wouldn't change any part of it.

When I was a little girl I loved going to shows and fairs and functions of that nature. I will confess that my main interest in these was the fairy floss! That pink, sticky, wonderfully sweet concoction was all I really craved at the Show, apart from a show bag which, when I was a kid, was worth buying.

I remember on my honeymoon being deliciously naughty and confessing my addiction to my new husband who quickly found a place we could go in order to satisfy my craving. Throughout the early years of our married life, I continued to enjoy it whenever a fairy floss machine could be found. It intrigued me the way it was made … … the way the operator controlled this wispy, cottonwool-looking confection and then presented it fresh and delightful to the purchaser. I could never feel complete approval when it was made and stored in parcels on a shelf.

However, as my three daughters have reached maturity anything sugary has brought forth their condemnation and if I confessed to my love of fairy floss, I could sense and see their disapproval. From then on, I ceased to even mention this love, and even felt guilty about my secret longing! There is no way I would have bought fairy floss when I was with them.

And so, for many years, I denied the craving ... ... until recently. At the beginning of the year a friend and I travelled to Dalgety in NSW to visit friends who ran the caravan park there. The Dalgety Show was on during our time there and I wondered aloud to my friend whether there would be a fairy floss stall operating.

Instead of scoffing, my friend said, "Oh I do hope so. I love fairy floss and haven't had it for years".

Her response was music to my ears and I confessed to my longing. I was amazed and delighted to hear that she too had avoided this delicacy for the same reason as mine. The next day, we found the fairy floss stall and watched the operator do his thing. No stored parcels there! We made our purchase and wandered contentedly enjoying the soft, sticky delicacy without any recriminations. It was sublime. We found a willing party to take our photo showing our enjoyment of just a little bit of naughtiness in our senior years – my friend in her seventies and yours truly in the eighties!

And we felt no guilt whatsoever.

Molly Smith

The Irish Influence

When the Rev. George Kingston, and his wife and four small children, migrated from Ireland in 1954 to settle in Denmark where he was to become the Rector of the Church of England Parish, the communities of Denmark and westwards had no idea of the impact this amazing man would have on their districts.

George Kingston was in his thirties. He was big in stature and in personality. In fact, you could almost say he took Denmark and its western areas by storm!

The Rev. Kingston travelled out to Walpole regularly and held Church services in the little Mission House that had moved from the Hazelvale district to its new position near where St George's Church Hall is today. However, where formerly Church Services had only attracted up to ten church goers, services with Rev. Kingston increased from time to time until fifty or sixty people eagerly made their way to hear his sermons. He welcomed all religions to his services and that fact endeared him to the community.

A new building was the obvious answer and, as George Kingston had building experience from his life in Ireland, he set to work to bring the dream of a new Church Hall to fruition. He became known as the "building parson". With this dynamic and inspirational man at the helm, the idea quickly became a reality.

Planning began in 1955 and, with the aid of a qualified carpenter in charge, building began in January 1956.

From then on donations of all forms of assistance flowed in. For example, the stumps were cut and split on a farmer's property from donated timber.

Equipment, vehicles and labour were all freely given and alongside the labouring community George Kingston could be found wielding a shovel or a handsaw.

George Kingston's motto was "when you want something done, ask the busiest person". The project was embraced by the whole community and, at the suggestion of the Rev. Kingston, many farmers donated the proceeds from the sale of a calf from their herd.

The building was opened in June 1956 (with the ceiling to be added later due to dwindling funds). There was a strong suggestion to name the hall Kingston Hall but, as the Rev. George declined this honour, it was named St George's Church Hall. A fitting tribute to this amazing man who became everybody's friend as well as a well-loved spiritual leader.

The Rev Kingston left the district in 1957 to work in Gosnells. He died in August 2013.

George Kingston also held services in the Tingledale Hall where again he was extremely popular. My memory of him was his regular arrival at the Hall, when he would hurry in, wiry hair standing on end, pull on his cassock (usually crumpled) and take his place at the front of the parishioners where his work boots could be seen peeping out from under the robe. Truly an amazing man who will long be remembered throughout the district.

Molly Smith

January 13th Walk

I walked a backward walk today,
Argued all the way
With wind and a wall of sand and grit
Which dared me to break through it.

Wind gusts whipped up black river water
Into tentacles which grasped my ankles,
Clunked and lifted boats and yachts
Blew a gale at a hundred knots.

Whirled its way through the café door,
Lifted the dust on the concrete floor,
Blended with the pungent smell
Of chips and steak on oil greased grill.

Whistled out from that dining house
To whet the palate of my mouth,
To make me stall, to make me stop
Outside that tantalizing shop.

At that moment my determination
To carry out my New Year's Resolution
To become fitter, my health to mind
Was damaged by that errant wind.

By the way I do not eat steak and chips!

Lorraine Spring

Let's Go for a Walk.

For just an instant our eyes met before we went our separate ways – she continued in one direction; I battled against the cold southerly wind blowing onto the sand. I forgot about her in my newfound pleasure of beach walking in this seaside town.

I moved here not long before the autumn weather set in. After the city summer heat, petrol fumes, and the flurry of workers, a walk along the beach onto the bay rocks thrilled me. Each time I went there, I lifted my head, breathed in the chilled, salt-laden wind. Within seconds my anxieties vanished.

It was on one of my evening wanderings that I saw her again, an attractive woman, barefoot, walking on the rocks.

She paused every few minutes to gaze out to sea before resuming her stroll. I saw her various times after that; tried to walk close enough to say hullo but, before I could reach her, she disappeared. At first, I thought she had walked around the headland and, of course, I would not see her on the other side. After the third or fourth time of trying to catch her and never succeeding, I asked about her in town.

'Oh, you have seen Bella.'

'Who is Bella?'

'Our ghost. Been walking the rocks for almost twenty years now, ever since her husband disappeared into the ocean. Never got over it, searched day and night; the beach, the tracks up the hill, even walked the roads into the farmlands.' The older folk recalled her well. 'She never came into town after her husband went, not to shop, nor to chat to anyone.'

Bella became a peculiarity.

'Months after her husband's disappearance, she found a piece of fabric washed up on the rocks. She recognized it, a piece of his shirt. That was when she disappeared. When people like you ask about the lady who walks the rocks, we know it's Bella looking for her husband.'

I listened, enthralled by this story. It hurt, like my story. I too had lost my lover, my partner, my husband, not because of an accident – no – through my stupidity of wanting to be the best in the powerful corporation in which I held the highest position. Oh, yes, we had the fineries, the house; the cars; the yacht; the holidays, all achieved by my continual work. What we did not have was the connection; he had his love of music, of art, of the natural world and I had my work.

Bella's story so touched me I went to the library, looked up old newspapers and found the reports about their disappearances. Yes, it was all two decades ago. She told the police that day, that sad and never-forgotten day, she had suggested they go for a walk, to which he replied he wanted to watch TV.

'It is such a lovely afternoon, far too nice to stay inside. Come on, get your sneakers on and we'll go down by the beach jetty, along the rocks.'

'I hate those rocks; they are too slippery.'

Even as a grown man he had a wariness of the rocks, knowing how quickly the sea waters could change – be calm one minute and a raging monster the next.

'We'll be fine. We'll walk together.'

He protested all the way as they drove the short distance to the beach. After parking, they strolled along the gleaming, white sands washed clean from the surge of the great Southern Ocean, its tides, and storms. They listened to the thunder of waves crashing on the shore and admired the surfers riding the waves from far out in the ocean depths.

'That was what I wanted to do as a kid.' Various articles mentioned his lost years in the army, gone from home as a teenager, returned after serving overseas, injured.

Newspapers reported that as dusk set in, the couple was last seen walking the rocks in the bay's corner, not long before a distraught woman ran into the coffee shop.

'My husband has gone, he's gone.' She'd collapsed sobbing as she reached the counter.

A search of the area by the staff could not find him. The woman sobbed. She had turned to fossick for shells wedged in rocks, but when she turned back, he had gone, not a sound, not a murmur Just gone.

Days and weeks passed; no one sighted the man. The police interviewed his wife several times, but her story never faltered. While they did not charge her, the talk around town was that she had done something bad.

After that, Bella walked the rocks every day searching, always searching. Not one sighting.

Her story so affected me, I began to write. I wrote of the love a woman once had for her husband. I wrote of the passion that filled her heart and his, and the sorrow they experienced when their child was stillborn. I wrote of the sacrifices he made to enable her to achieve a high status in her work position. Occasionally, she apologised for leaving him at home while she attended one function after another, all in the name of improving their lives. And I wrote of her misery when he disappeared.

I read through my scribbles, thinking I was writing about Bella and her husband; I had, instead, written my story, the story of my marriage and a husband who'd decided it was pointless to stay in a union made up of materials. He did not tell me he was leaving.

I searched through further newspapers, found that the day she discovered a piece of shirt washed up on the rocks where he had vanished, was the last time anybody saw her.

Over the following years, Bella was often seen wandering the rocks, walking up and down, every so often stopping to gaze out to sea. 'It's her ghost.' The townspeople assured me she meant no harm, just walked, constantly looking for her man. Some said, she never forgave herself for not watching him and the treacherous waves.

I finished my writing; felt more rested than I had been for many months.

The next time I went to the beach, I walked on the rocks where Bella's husband had disappeared.

As I climbed over the rocky outcrops, I saw in the distance a figure, a woman, Bella, but now she had with her a man. Together they held hands, walked towards me, passed by, looked in my direction then disappeared into the water. For an instant, her eyes met mine, and I saw in hers compassion for me.

That was the last time I saw her but not the last time I walked the rocks in that town. My heart regained a measure of peace that day. I knew I could never bring my marriage back, but I lived and hoped.

Lorraine Spring

Seeking Adventure

At the tender age of eighteen, I left the comforting shores of Northern England to work as a Nanny in New Jersey. My American Green Card (work visa) was for twelve months. After five months of 12-hour days, with one begrudged day off a week, I'd had enough of being the Maid/Nanny/Cook. One day my three-year-old charge threw her puppy down the stairs and broke its back. To cheer her up, her over-indulgent parents promised to buy her a new puppy. I knew it was time to leave.

As they had advanced my plane fare, I put the exact amount in an envelope and left it on the bed in my basement room. Late that night, using a chair, I climbed up through the storm window. Despite the snow covering the ground, I walked several miles to the nearest bus stop, having worried they would try to have my visa cancelled if I told them I was leaving. I was not only ignorant of the laws about visas, but had no one to ask – *Google* being many years into the future.

Fortune favoured me: the bus took me to New York, and the driver pointed me to a nearby women's backpacker hostel. I spent the following week there, checking out the *New York Times* every day for work. One ad caught my eye – 'No experience necessary – we train – great wages for young people from overseas.'

Using the hostel pay phone, I phoned the number, and they told me to come for an interview that afternoon. The run-down office in an equally run-down part of Manhattan should have warned me. How delighted I was when I got the job – even more so when they said I would start the next day. (Did I mention I was a naïve eighteen-year-old?)

Early the next morning, a pale green van picked me up outside the hostel. Inside, I joined five other people, scrunched up together on the carpeted floor. Once the door slid closed behind me, the van took off at a speed that threw us all against each other.

Over the next three hours, we got to know each other pretty well – easy to do when your elbow is in someone's face and a pair of feet rest on your back. No one seemed to mind – and I certainly wasn't rocking the boat – I was off on an American Adventure at last!

When we finally stopped outside a shabby motel block, the driver told us to climb out. Cramped muscles ached as we crawled from the van and followed him into the motel lobby. He sorted us into three pairs, gave each a key to a room, and then told us to meet him in the motel diner in fifteen minutes.

Laura, my 'partner', took our key and we bolted to our room – a much-needed toilet break first on the list. The room came as no surprise – dingy, though clean. The two single beds had enough space to edge over to the tiny bathroom.

When we entered the diner later, our driver told us to order whatever we liked as the firm footed the bill. Of course, we made the most of it, cramming our mouths with greasy burgers and chips. During the meal, no one spoke, but as soon as we had finished, the driver told us we would begin our 'work' the next morning.

"We have had no training yet," Laura said, but the driver held up his hand as everyone else murmured in agreement.

"There is only one thing to remember. You are all overseas students, on study visas, trying to earn money to continue your studies at NYU."

This is when the alarm bells should have rung. The glib-talking driver quickly filled the stunned silence. He gave us more instructions on how we were to go about our new careers, leaving us little time to take it all in. After we knock on the door, we must first compliment the householder on their beautiful home. Before they had time to answer, we introduce ourselves as a hard-working overseas student. After a chat about the lack of education in our own country, we sign them up for an annual magazine subscription. Finally, we had learned about our 'exciting' new career—door-to-door magazine subscription selling.

Meals and instructions ended, and we went back to our rooms to practice our speeches on each other.

As soon as our motel door closed, Laura said we should get out of here as soon as possible. She didn't like the sound of this. Why did they not tell us about the job before we left New York?

Reluctant to give up on my American Adventure, I talked her into staying, at least for the next few days. The rest of the evening passed by practising our speeches on each other. After a while, we couldn't go on as we kept giggling and saying ridiculous things, so we gave up and went to bed.

The next morning, after an early breakfast, everyone piled into the van. The driver dropped us off in pairs at intervals along separate streets. Before we left, our driver reminded us not to say we were selling magazine subscriptions.

"Keep the conversation away from that until the end," he said.

Laura murmured from behind, "Yes, like you did to us."

The driver, ignoring her, said he would pick us up in an hour's time and handed us order pads with a pen attached.

We were the last pair to leave the van. Laura was to take the left of the street and I was to knock on doors on the right side. The houses lay some distance apart, sprawling buildings with manicured gardens. I started up the first path, past life-sized stone statues of flamingos and deer. When I reached the wide oak door, I hesitated before giving a few quick knocks.

After a pause, which to me seemed like hours, the double door opened a crack. A young woman holding a toddler in her arms looked out.

"Hello, can I help you?" she asked. Behind her, I could see an entrance hall covered in thick shag carpet. Gilded mirrors and pictures decorated the wallpapered walls. This was a place I could say to her in all honesty, "What a beautiful home you have," and my speech could carry on from there.

Instead, I blurted out, "I am selling magazine subscriptions," and she shut the door in my face. Startled, I did not know why she had reacted like that, so I knocked on the door again. This time, she opened the door a few inches. I asked her why she had shut the door on me before I had said anything else.

"What you are doing, young lady, is a scam – one the authorities warned us against. After we have paid for a year's subscription, the magazines never arrive. The company changes its name and address, so we have no chance of recovering our money."

Horrified, I apologised as she closed the door on me again. Across the street, I saw Laura heading my way. She, too, had met with the same reaction. We agreed not to repeat the humiliation of knocking on another door. Together, we walked towards the end of the street to wait for the van. As we had about an hour to kill, we sat on an ornate bench at the end of someone's garden and discussed our options. Neither of us wanted to remain in this 'career' a second longer. First, though, we must collect our belongings from the motel. To be honest, we did not know where we were, not even street-smart Laura. The many dubious lanes and alleyways of New York City were her home, but here she admitted to being lost.

By the time the van arrived, we had made our plans. After

dinner (we weren't so stupid as to leave on an empty stomach) we would say we were going for a walk. Then we would hitch a ride to the nearest bus station. As plans go, it was full of holes, but without transport or any idea where we were, we had little choice.

The van driver was not happy that neither of us had any orders, but several of the others had managed a few. He put it down to first-time nerves and said we'd do better tomorrow. As we had no intention of being there the next day, we nodded our agreement. Silence reigned for the ride back to the motel.

Our escape went without a hitch. The main road was close to the motel, and the first car that stopped pointed us to a nearby bus stop down the street. Assured the bus for New York often came past, we sat on our packs and waited. Within the hour, a blue Greyhound bus pulled up. Between us, we scraped up the fare, and several hours later, alighted at the bus terminal in New York.

"Come home with me," Laura said. "I live with my mother in the Projects and she'll be happy to see you." The locals called the area Laura lived in those towering blocks of flats, Spanish Harlem.

Laura's mother made me welcome, and I lived with them for the next seven months until my visa ended. I made no more forays into the world of selling. Instead, I worked in an office in Manhattan as an NCR Accounting Machine Operator, the same job I had in England. The rest of my stay then became the American Adventure I'd dreamed of.

Two years later, Laura and I met up in Denmark and travelled around Europe on mopeds with tents bundled on the back. But that is another adventure!

Laura and I in her brother's jackets being 'Beatles'.

Laura playing guitar.

Wendy Stackhouse

The Angel with High Heels

Azekiel looked across the room at the seraphim's feet.

"High Heels?" he thundered. "Is this your idea of modern angel attire, or have you decided to join the rest of the fallen?"

The junior angel trembled as the head of the Power angels loudly voiced his displeasure.

"Please don't send me down to earth again," the youngster begged. "I can't go among the humans anymore. Their wicked thoughts hurt my head, and I never found a single one deserving of wings. Neither could I send them through the gates for you to assess for entrance to the Throne."

"That is not your place to decide," Azekiel said, his all-seeing eyes burning into hers. "The Throne gave me, and me alone, the duty of deciding who was worthy of entrance, and who deserved wings. When you have shown sufficient maturity and good judgement, you will be tasked with wing allocation."

He made a point of staring fixedly at the bright red high heels she was trying unsuccessfully to tuck beneath the chair, before continuing again in the same thunderous tones.

"Explain to me why you have returned to us before your allotted time on earth with those abominations on your feet?"

By now, the seraphim had decided honesty, especially to such a high-ranking Power as Azekiel, was the best and only policy. After gulping in a large amount of celestial air, she looked down at the offending footwear and sighed.

"When you sent me down to learn my craft, I found myself in a land of unusual animals and even stranger people. Red soil covered the ground as far as the eye could see, and sweat trickled permanently down my neck. As we are not allowed to manifest our wings when on assignment, I had to find another way to travel towards a place where people dwelled, in order to make my assessments. All morning I trudged through thick dust until a huge truck pulled alongside me and the driver slowed to a stop.

"'Hop in, girlie'," he called down, 'You will die of thirst before you get to where you're going.'

"Grateful, I climbed into the seat next to him and the rest of my journey was accomplished in air-conditioned comfort.

"'Where are you heading?' the driver asked as the heavy vehicle sped down a dirt road, sending red dust flying past the windows.

"I didn't know what to answer, so mumbled "Town" as by now I could read his thoughts which were getting more suspicious by the moment. I doubted he could figure out who I was, but knew he was wondering how on earth I came to be out in the middle of the desert, on my own, with little sign of sunburn or dehydration. I avoided enlightening him as much as I could, knowing this was part of my test.

"When the truck rumbled into a large yard on the outskirts of town, I slid from the seat before he could ask any more awkward questions, and headed towards a wide street in the town centre. Women filled the pathways, many wearing the same shoes you see on me now. In order to blend in, I went to the nearest shoe store and bought this pair. When I continued my walk along the street near the other women, I read the awful thoughts of not only the women but the men who stopped frequently to talk to them:

"'Don't know where she sprung from, but if she doesn't get off my patch she'll wake up with a split head.'

"'Little tart. I'll make sure she doesn't steal any of my johnnies.'

"'She's a looker. What I couldn't do with her!'

"By now I knew there was little I could accomplish here. These people had nothing but sin on their minds, each and every one of them. I decided to leave as soon as I could get around a corner and free my wings. As I rounded the next corner, I glanced at the road sign. 'Hay Street, Kalgoorlie'."

Instead of admonishing her as she now expected, Azekiel threw back his head and laughed, his great shoulders shaking with unaccustomed mirth.

"Oh, little seraphim," he said as she turned a puzzled face towards him. "You have a lot to learn about the land of men!"

Wendy Stackhouse

The title of this story was a writing prompt given as an example of Speculative Fiction.

A Nod and a Smile!

A nod and a smile!
Give me the sense of warm greetings
Represent the peace in the Nile
Provide me with lots of meanings

A nod and a smile!
Set the feeling of acceptance
If hurt, it may reduce my bile
Change my mood in just an instance

A nod and a smile!
A message of acknowledgement
Treasure it in my mental file
for positive encouragement

A nod and a smile!
How powerful the sense could be!
Reach great achievement by that style
Vivid sense of love I could see

Chelsea Whitfield

Preoccupied with False Assumption

Carol didn't understand how time slipped from her fingers so fast. She was shocked to see herself reach forty. She just celebrated her fortieth birthday. She knew if she didn't do anything, she would never meet someone she might fall in love with. A few days later when she bumped into Sally in Sunter Shopping Centre, they agreed to have an impromptu lunch together. At the far end table at the food court, they sat down side by side. After they finished their food, Carol couldn't wait to share her thoughts with Sally.

"Carol! You know, my birthday wish this year was to get a good husband," Sally said excitedly. They were so close they talked about everything.

"What? To get a husband?"

Carol lowered her voice and told Sally discreetly, "I have reached forty and may miss the chance of getting married if I don't do it now. I asked my relatives in Perth to help me with the matchmaking."

"Wow! Do you still believe in that? Will you let others determine the big decision of marriage?"

"Why not? It's worth trying. It'd be better than doing nothing."

Sally shrugged. It was Carol's life.

The following month, Auntie June in Perth called Carol. "Carol, I've been trying to see if there's anyone suitable for you. It so happened that my neighbour, a widower with two adult children, was looking for a wife. His name is Adrian. When I asked him what type of lady he was looking for, he described it and I think you are the most suitable one. I showed him your photo and told him a bit about you. He seemed interested. How about you? I just sent through his photo to you. Please have a look and let me know whether you're interested in seeing him?"

Carol took a look at the photo. Adrian was not a handsome guy, but his eyes looked tender and compassionate. She liked him.

"Yes, I am. How could we meet?"

"He's very keen to see you. If you agree, he'll fly to Jakarta to meet you."

"That'll be perfect."

"However, you have to bear in mind that since it's a long-distance way of courting, you should prepare yourself to get married soon and move to Perth if everything goes smoothly." Her Auntie listed the potential hurdles lying ahead, the adjustment that she should prepare herself to face. She believed she could handle it.

"Yes, I will."

*****

Two months later, Carol called Sally.

"Guess what? I'm going to get married at the end of this month."

"Hah! Are you sure? You're going to marry someone you hardly know!"

"Yes, I'm sure. This is the only chance I've got."

"Have you considered the consequences?" Sally was shocked.

"Yes, I've already talked about almost everything with my Auntie."

"You shouldn't be that desperate! You're pretty, kind-hearted, energetic and full of compassion. Some white horse prince must be somewhere waiting to marry you," Sally joked.

"Don't you remember my age? I've already passed my youth. My opportunity is very rare."

"I don't think a woman should get married until she finds her soulmate. It's not a problem at all that she stays single nowadays. Marriage is not the only solution for women. There are many options in life. She can have a career and be financially independent."

"I understand that. However, this is a golden opportunity. If I don't grasp it, I'll lose it."

"Why do you regard it as a golden opportunity?"

"Of course! You see, he is an Australian citizen."

"So, what has that to do with your marriage?" Sally asked, puzzled.

"If I marry him, I would get a spousal bridging visa which later on would become a Permanent Resident visa."

"Why do you relate your marriage to the Permanent Resident?" Sally still couldn't make head nor tail of her thinking. To her, marriage should be carried out because of love, not visa.

"You're too naive!" Carol sighed, trying to explain it to her friend. "By marrying him, I could get a visa and stay in Australia forever. It's a good thing for me to do. I can work there and earn Australian dollar."

"I believe we should get married for love, not for other reasons. You deserve someone who truly loves you and that you love too. This way, you'll live an emotionally happy life."

"He has fallen in love with me. He visited me several times. We went out for dinner. We chatted through FaceTime almost every night. He tried to explain to me Perth's way of life. He said that I still need to learn a lot of things, such as driving and studying English."

"Do you really love him?"

"I will love my husband! Love will grow gradually."

"Assure me: did you like him at the start?"

"Yes, I did. He's a nice man. He's kind and polite. He told me he lost his wife a year ago. When he mentioned his wife, I could see the tears that he fought back."

"Ooo, I see. If you truly like him, hopefully, it will turn into love; I shouldn't be concerned too much then. However, you need to be aware that it could be hard for you to marry someone that you haven't adjusted to yet. On top of that, you're going to live in a foreign country that you're not familiar with. It could be a challenge for you to adjust."

"Thank you for your kind advice. Don't worry! I know I can settle down well, with him. My Auntie who's living in Perth will always support me."

"Nonetheless, if there's anything that you need my help with, please feel free to call, especially now that we've got Whatsapp. Free call, which is good! I honour your decision and I'll bless you!"

Sally had known Carol for such a long time. As Carol was a woman of her word, she would keep her word to love her husband besides her desire to get a visa; Sally could tell.

At the end of the month, Carol and Adrian were married. He applied for her visa and stayed temporarily in Jakarta until she received her temporary spousal visa and moved to Australia and lived with him for good. Was it happily ever after?

*****

It was Sunday. Sally was watching the news on television when her mobile phone started ringing. She picked it up without looking at the caller ID.

"Hi, Sally! It's Carol."

"Huh? Are you in Jakarta?"

"Yes, I am!" Her voice cracked, then turned into sobbing.

"What happened? Is anything wrong?"

"It's a long story. Can we meet now?

"Sure! Where can we meet? I'll cancel my plan to go grocery shopping."

"McDonalds on Thamrin Road."

*****

As soon as Sally arrived, she went over to Carol, who had already ordered them snacks and drinks.

"Let me have a good look at you! You look slimmer, but firmer." Sally tried to reduce the obvious tension on Carol's face.

"It's really hard for me to survive there. I'm going to give up. I was too naive to believe that marriage is between a man and a woman. I hadn't realised there is a whole lot of family members and relatives who would be interfering in our lives, especially from his late wife's side. He's still maintained the Indonesian custom and culture," Carol revealed instantly.

"What do you mean? Are there any other family members living with you? Or are they visiting occasionally?"

"I live with two of his adult children, one male, one female. As Indonesians, the father lets them stay at home even though they are working now. It doesn't matter if they live together in harmony. The problem is that they always have such an intense animosity toward me – as if I've taken away their father from their mother, or their house from them. They cynically criticise me all the time, as if I came from a village and knew nothing at all about Western culture."

"Mmm…" Sally looked at her sympathetically.

"They put up their late mother's huge framed photo in front of the dining room, giving the impression that it's her house, not mine. When I happened to be around, they would stop chatting about other things and purposely talked about her in front of me, stressing all her goodness. They would compare the food their mother prepared and said how good it was and how delicious it was. They would mention how the mother cleaned the floor, washed the clothes, or anything that they could think of. If they did it inadvertently, it didn't matter. However, they did it on purpose with the intent to hurt my feeling or, if possible, to get rid of me. They always stressed that it's their parents' house and I should never think of getting their house. I have tried to be patient until I can stand it no more. I think I have had enough. So I came back without any plan of going back to Perth. I just give up everything."

"From what I've just heard, do you mean that they couldn't take you in as you've become a threat for them to lose the house they are living in?"

"Yes, it could be the case."

"I could see from your story that no matter how hard you tried, you couldn't possibly make peace with them, as it concerns the inheritance that they would supposedly get from their father after he dies, and now you have become the obstacle."

"I figured that could be the case. That's why I suggested Adrian sell the house and move to a smaller house, but he declined as he thought that it's his own, or that it's his hard-earned property, and he deserved it. If the children were not happy, they may move out."

"The worst part was that they tried to influence their other family members from both sides, I mean, from their father's side and their mother's side – all to side with them. As most of them have got the adverse image of me, that either the children have created or the stigma of a 'stepmother', whatever I do or say would mean nothing – they always hold on to the false assumption and image. So I become the 'evil' or 'bad' stepmother no matter what truth is shown to them. Since my arrival there, I have been trying so hard to fulfil my role as a good wife, but to them, I am just as bad as Cinderella's stepmother. Everything I do or say is nothing to them. To them, it's a pretence."

"Can't any of their family members have the conscience to be able to discern 'right' from 'wrong'? How could they just believe and follow whatever the two adults said? To me, a good decent person or a gentleman should be able to stand up for the right matters, but not just side with the person that they love without reasoning. I have never imagined that this bad influence, this 'evil strategy', could happen to you. It's sad!"

"Have you seen this kind of thing before?"

"Yes. Whenever a threat sets in, some people become defensive to protect what they claim to be theirs. Their sinful nature comes to the surface and they do everything they can to protect their belongings. For example, someone's rice bowl. I think it's just a survival instinct. People basically are sinful."

"That's what is happening to me now. It's so hurtful. It's already hard for me to adjust to and tolerate my husband in a foreign country. Moreover, I have to adjust to his two children and all of their family members. It's just too much for me. You didn't see how hostile they were towards me."

"It seems to me that you've got more responsibilities after marriage than before and you have experienced more hardship."

"Absolutely!"

"That's why I always believe that no matter what status you are in, either single or married, we should just be content about it. Living in this world itself isn't easy, let alone living with another sinful man. No matter what our status is, we just live and enjoy each day as we can."

"I can see it clearly now." Carol smiled sheepishly.

"Okay, let's drop this subject for a while. Tell me! Now that you have lived there for nearly a year, have you got any close friends there?"

"Unfortunately, no! I can't find a close friend as I have here. Apart from the busy house chores I have to do, I also go to study in TAFE and work as a 'night filler' in one of the supermarkets there to refill the shelves at night. I am so busy that I have no time for a new friend."

"Ooo, that's not good."

"I don't think Perth residents would like to make friends with me with our Asian habits and customs."

"What do you mean?"

"For instance, they organise well their plans and schedules. Today I called you out just like that, and you would adjust your schedule for me without any feeling of getting offended. You are happy to meet up with me just like this, and might cancel your original plan as you appreciate our friendship as such."

"When in Rome, do as the Romans do. You should follow their culture by making a plan and following through as much as you can."

"I agree."

"Friendship does need time and effort to build. You should work on it."

"That's right. I always love to meet with genuine and trustworthy friends. What a treasure!"

"Give yourself time and I'm sure you'll find them."

"Finger-crossed." Carol smiled, crossing her fingers.

*****

A month later, Adrian flew to Jakarta. After Carol's departure, he realised how devoted she was to the family and how much she had served his family without any complaints. He missed her so much. After considering her suggestion of selling the house, he came to realise that it was a good decision for maintaining their relationship. So, he prepared himself for the move and put the house on the market through a real estate agent, despite his children's objections. By downsizing his house, he could give some money to his children for a deposit on their own houses. Once the decision was made, he felt truly relieved. On arriving in Jakarta, he discussed things with Carol and took her back to Perth.

Chelsea Whitfield

Genuine Love's all that Matters

Your true love happiest wedding day!
No huge celebration entailed
No bounty of beverage or drinks
No splendid venue to present
Just loving family and friends
to wish you a merry marriage

The brilliant beauty of nature is displayed
above the lectern, the priest stood
Not due to your perfect posture
Nor the grandeur of the venue
Nor the great many of your guests
Nor the grand mouth-watering food

The camera captured wondrously
the aesthetic and artistic scenic view
of the volatile floating white clouds
so stunningly stretching out
dancing over the clear blue sky

Predestined by some hidden Hands?
The Creator of the universe
bestowed on you this unique view
the impressive image that'll last
What a blissful, blessed wedding!
showing genuine love is all that matters

Chelsea Whitfield

The Sea

The Sea, the beach, the white sand under our feet. It's so amazing! Time fled so fast! It was two years ago, wasn't it? The time when Isabel and I were still together enjoying the beautiful sunset, sitting side by side, holding hands. Occasionally exchanging affectionate gazes, I could still feel the loving atmosphere, so deeply engraved in my mind that no matter how hard I had been trying, her smiling image, her mesmerising eyes, would never leave its space in some part of my mind.

Winston was late. To pass the time, I gazed at the sea. It was so calm and tranquil! Occasionally it sent out the frolicking waves, one over another, hitting the beach with naughty bubbles. If only it had the same gentle waves that day. That very day! We might possibly have been married and had two children by now.

Winston and I were having our monthly catch-up at Cicerello's. I ordered fish and chips and he ordered his favourite dish of raw oysters and grilled Barramundi. After our meals, we both ordered Chamomile Tea.

Again I gazed at the sea. It was now getting dark. I didn't want to miss the last drop of light before it was all covered by total darkness.

"Thinking of Isabel, Edward?" His empathy was obvious.

"…" Nothing came out of my mouth. I could hear the sound of the waves hitting rocks somewhere out there. Some things used to be familiar.

"She's in a better place now," Winston said in a soft voice.

"It's so hard to believe that she's gone." Tears filled my eyes.

"Yeah … but the fact is, she's no more in this world."

"I should have saved her." I couldn't hide the agony in my voice.

"You were trying to save her, but you would have ended up dying with her. The waves were unbelievably high. If not for the photographer and us holding you tightly, you might have also jumped into the sea. No way! It's impossible for you to help her in that instance. You should be realistic," Edward blurted out.

"Mmm. At that very moment, all I had in mind was to save her. I couldn't think of the risk to myself anymore." My mind reached out further to that shocking moment.

"Yeah … I understand. That's just the response of your love."

"…" I sighed.

"Now that you have taken this in, you shouldn't blame yourself anymore."

"I know! I must have passed the stage of blaming game."

"How about your anger? Are you still angry at the incident? Angry with the fate? Angry with God?"

"I'm not sure. I remember I was terribly angry about the incident. I asked God why it had happened to her?"

"It seemed that you had accepted the fact that she was gone. It was your grieving that had been disturbing you, wasn't it?"

"You could be right. In order to understand this grieving process, I went for counselling. It helped me understand … helped me a lot in coping with my grief."

"That's good to hear." Winston stared at me, full of sympathy.

"Still, her image always appears in my imaginary view." I needed to get it off my chest.

"Come on, Edward! You need to move on. She could be listening to you. If she could feel your in-depth sadness as such, she wouldn't be happy," he said matter of factly.

"I didn't realise that I loved her so deeply until I lost her. Just a month before our wedding! Could you imagine that? We shouldn't have had our pre-wedding photos done at Anyar Beach, no matter how much we loved that beach."

"But nobody could predict that Tsunami would rise out of nowhere."

"Of course not, no warning whatsoever. The meteorology must have had some information but they didn't announce anything to the public." I was about to fall into the blaming game again.

"What has happened can't be undone. Have you ever thought that if the one who was swept away by the huge wave was you, what then would you like Isabel to do instead?" Winston gazed at me, waiting for my response.

"It has never occurred to me like that." The thought struck me.

"Just imagine that! How would you want her to live?" Winston insisted, challenging me to look at it from a different angle.

"Of course, I want her to be happy and move on with her life. I would wish her joyfully serving God, or doing any job she could get that she loved."

"Let's say that if you were in heaven enjoying the afterlife with God, what would you like her to do? Think of it specifically!"

I thought for a while.

"I would like her to stop grieving, perhaps get another boyfriend, get married and move on with her life in a blissful manner."

"That's exactly what I have in mind. You should let her go! Let her get out of your mind! I mean it's okay for you to think of her once in a while with no pain involved. No matter what will happen in the future, you should move on. Besides, your tasks and responsibilities in your job require your full concentration. A wife would do you all good if God blessed you a wise one!"

Again, I was trying to look at the beach, but there was nothing I could see as it was quite dark. Nothing! Was it due to the darkness? Was it gone? Disappeared? The non-existence would sustain no significant meaning anymore. Should I look for something tangible at this point in time?

Chelsea Whitfield

Healing

The ancient meaning of the word 'heal' is whole, holiness, oneness. The key element that unites all forms of healing is unconditional love and compassion, as healing is not only for the body but must serve the mind as in belonging and caring. When the body becomes the major concern of the mind, then the mind cannot fulfil its potential. True healing is expressed in the mind of the healer and has a lasting effect on the body of the client. It is helping others to get back on the path of harmony and balance. It is a learning experience for the healer, a process where the client and healer heal each other's pain in a never-ending process.

It is a fact that people who are diseased in body recover and heal quicker if they can love themselves. Love is the most significant thing in human life and given of a person's free will. When we choose to love, it comes from within, our deepest essence is felt by others and has a physical effect, not just an emotional experience but a whole-body experience. Stress and illness are usually caused by a combination of things – physical, mental and emotional. Healing is a positive feedback system, illness a form of negative feedback. Health or wholeness is our natural state; sometimes we lose the power to take charge of our own well-being. Healing removes obstructions that block this state, gives power to the client embracing them with energy and positive vibrations, exciting them to get their own energy, stimulating them to become aware of the flow of energy in their own body.

Honesty and truthful self-discovery are required to experience permanent recovery and spiritual growth. Listen to the inner voice of wisdom and find truth. With intention and practice, we can learn to control our mind, which brings the deepest healing and victory over suffering, a place where the mind is at peace. Inner silence through meditation can bring us to a state of expanded awareness producing lasting positive effects. Healing is natural: everyone has the capacity to heal; we do it with each other without being aware, of the process and journey of life. Effective healing does not come from increased education or mastery of techniques, but rather from when we open our heart and spirit to the gifts we already possess.

Sheila Williamson

Holistic Healing

Purify the air: burn pine, basil, juniper, rosemary, cedarwood, camphor with citrus.

Illness strikes when body, mind and spirit are out of harmony. Ask questions about past medical history: any chronic complaints like asthma, eczema etc. Ask if they have suffered a serious illness, accident or injury. Ask questions about nutrition and lifestyle and whether they smoke or drink excessively. Is it stress-related? Ask the patient to describe symptoms, and any physical manifestations. How are the bowel movements?

Physical health reflects what is happening on a deeper level. When you need help, you must ask for it. Pray for strength; have faith – a journey is always hardest in the middle. Love and accept your body; you are a special unique individual. Your mind powers are in the nerve centres, the energy: your thoughts can heal your body. See sickness as an opportunity to rest. A cold or diarrhoea is good cleansing, muscle pain a time for massage or soaking in a hot tub. Sinus could be tears that need to flow. See the ailment as an indication of growth, not an obstacle.

Colours, music and aromas can all help healing as they all affect the body's energy patterns.

Healing comes quicker if we understand our body's strengths and weaknesses and how stress affects them.

Whether the illness is physical, emotional or psychological, let the patient talk and listen to them. Ask them to create a metaphor for the illness. With this concrete image, the healer can construct a ceremony to fight it.

Before starting a healing, ask the patient three questions:

Who are you?

Where did you come from?

Why are you here?

We create our own world. What we believe in is what comes true. If there is enthusiasm in the heart, the feet will dance, and if you believe it, the body will heal.

An antispasmodic to relieve stress and tension: Valerian, Black Cohosh, Chamomile; there are also nervines, also Hypericum, and Skullcap.

Sheila Williamson

IATROGENIC = a disease caused by medicine — bad medicine.

About

The Society of Women Writers WA

The Society of Women Writers was first established in Australia in Sydney in September 1925, to bring together women writers and journalists in New South Wales. Their aims were to be a social body; to promote knowledge of literature; to encourage women writers; and to strengthen the ties of interest between Australian and visiting writers.

Until the 1970s, the Society was based in Sydney, using a postal critiquing system to keep in touch. During this decade, branches were established in other Australian states and the first Federal Constitution was adopted in 1978 with an agreement that Federal responsibility be transferred from state to state every two years. Twenty years later, the decision was made to decentralise, with each state forming its own Society.

The WA branch initially operated only through correspondence groups until the first President, Ethel Webb, was appointed in 1981 and members began to meet regularly. The Society of Women Writers WA was incorporated as an autonomous body on 25 February 2000.

Contact Details
The Society of Women Writers WA
PO Box 434
Northbridge
Western Australia 6865
Tel: 0415 840 031
Email: swwofwa@gmail.com
Web: www.swwofwa.com.au